The Silence of the Pain is Deafening

My Story

Marian "Pat" Benedict
Cmdr. USN NC Ret.

The Silence of the Pain is Deafening

My Story

By Marian "Pat" Benedict
Cmdr. USN NC Ret.

Copyright © 2016 Marian Marie Benedict
All rights reserved
ISBN 13: 978- 1540362810
      10: 1540352817

Edited by Steve Keller
www.paliggenesia.com

Contents

Forward	5
The early years	21
Childhood	41
Recollections and Reflections	59
Nursing	79
Africa: A Call to Serve and to Learn	107
The USS Repose Naval Hospital	151
Vietnam: A Brief History	195
Alcoholism: My Prison Within My Soul	235
Treatment: The Click that Unlocked the Lock	249
Friends are a Gift of Sobriety	263
Death Row	293
Epilogue	351

The Silence of the Pain is Deafening

Some time ago I read a comment made by Mahatma Gandhi that stuck in my head. He said he did not understand why people who call themselves Christians do not live as Christians. I think that this kind of hypocrisy, which is common to human nature, is something I should write about, and that is one of the reasons why I want to tell my life story.

There are common hypocrisies which, for most people, can be amplified by chronic alcohol use. Before I got sober my life was filled with duplicity. I would feel one way and yet speak and act as if I felt another way. I would cry when I should have laughed; I would be silent when I should have cried out. Through an examination of my life, I want to present an examination of the human condition, both in light of ourselves and in light of God. Also, I want to present and examine the typical effects of chronic alcohol use.

Most of us know that life is unfair, and yet we have been taught the contradictory proposition that all people are created equal. Most of us were taught that we can make our lives whatever we want them to be, as if we can change our characters to match a vision of the right way to live. We can talk about changing, but talk is cheap.

Changing our thought patterns and our behaviors is a most difficult endeavor. We are not all created equal. We are created as different individuals with our own personal strengths and

Forward

abilities. We develop our philosophies and our outlooks in response to our experiences. Some people have the ability to find strength within themselves so as to stand on their own two feet. Those people are able to strive for their highest happiness. Others of us may remain stagnant and miserable in this life. Civilizations experience times of war and times of peace; similarly, we individuals experience times of internal light and times of darkness. Individuals may live entire lives of misery or happiness. For many, life has both times of misery and times happiness. Few of us have the ability to change these things about ourselves.

 Years ago I heard a minister preaching about the 'psychology of life.' He offered his television congregation an exposition of the meaning of spirituality. He said, "Pick up your cross and follow me. Raise your spirits and think positive." Jesus did say, "Take up your cross and follow me." But nowhere does the Bible promote the 'powers of positive thinking.' This empty message rang in my ear for days. I became angry and wrote a letter to this televangelist: "Why don't you go to Ethiopia and tell the people who are starving to 'think positive?' Tell those emaciated children to get their bony little feet moving and pull their lives together. Make them understand that– despite their impoverished lives– they have to get on with their pathetic, devastated existence!" I was

Marian "Pat" Benedict Cmdr. USN NC Ret.

appalled to hear this master manipulator exclude most of the people on this planet from 'his people.' He built false hopes for those who supported his ministry, while his unspoken message was that life is fair for those who have money and power. The fact is people are not equal and life is not fair. There is little most of us can do about it: despite background, wealth or beauty; despite how good a person one is, life simply is what it is and not whatever we wish it to be. Life is not fair for the parents whose child is born with hydrocephalus (water on the brain). Life is not fair when a child is born blind. These children are not born equal to other children. And life is not fair for the children who are victims of incest or child abuse.

However, it is the way we perceive our lives and how we approach them that can make them worthwhile. It is my belief that we learn from negative experiences. We must see the darkness and hear the deafening silence before we are able to hear the trumpets blaring in the morning light. Helen Keller accomplished much in her life, supported as she was by her belief in the strength of the light within. She has been an inspiration to others. She believed that we should achieve what we can from what gifts we have; she believed in doing well for its own sake, without seeking gratification or rewards. I think she was (as all of us are) an instrument in God's plan.

My Story

Forward

In order to maintain my sanity, I do not question what I have made of my life. I believe that– given the opportunity– anyone, anywhere, at any time can work for and obtain whatever God intended for them. People can attain happiness and find fulfillment in their daily lives, even if they experience pain and tears with every step forward. Adversity can be turned into triumph, but first we must experience both negative and positive states of being on every level: physically, emotionally and spiritually. By expanding our consciousness through experience, we can realize our full potential. And so, to that end, we should explore all aspects of human experience; that is: the good and the bad.

Many of us go through life unfeeling and numb; hiding our deepest emotions– even from ourselves. Day by day society seems to grow colder and less humane. Analysis and worldly knowledge are held in the highest regard, while compassion and kindliness are trampled over on busy street corners. God and the higher powers within us are somehow lost in the shadows of society's values. A withdrawn hostility lingers in people's eyes and echoes from their empty words.

How could it be possible to have missed the entire reason for living? We come into this world alone, and we will leave this world alone, but in between we are here with others. While we are here, our focus should be on one another. Many of us

Marian "Pat" Benedict Cmdr. USN NC Ret.

forget where we came from and where we will return; for many, it is as if we just popped into this animated life situation from nowhere, and we are only obligated to ourselves.

Sometimes when I contemplate such cosmic concepts, it seems like the deeper I go, the less I understand. Sometimes I actually wonder what I'm thinking and where I'm going with it. So I will write about God, the beauty of life and my darkest hell, because I feel a desperate need to express my feelings from deep inside.

Through prayer I can relate to my Master. But such prayers aren't the way to relate to other people. So to my family, friends and peers, I am sending my prayers through this book. This book lists gifts and lessons which I have gathered from life. I hope it will touch other people and, at least for some, make their lives more acceptable or more understandable. To write this book without the guidance from the Master would be like painting without sunlight or acting without a script or director.

Often a story is told at a time and place when the storyteller feels the need to give expression to inner feelings. My life story cannot be told without expressing inner feelings. From the time I was born, my feelings have been both strong and poignant. Particularly strong feelings are more difficult to convey to other human beings. So where do I reach for a

My Story

Forward

beginning? I stretch my hand out to God for His light and words. I try to be open to the luminescence. Almost all of my successes in life were achieved in part by focusing on the spiritual. It was my contemplative side, my spiritual side, which helped me move myself up despite great obstacles.

As I have journeyed, sometimes I wondered why I didn't fall through the holes of life. I struggled, making things complicated. But now I realize that life was meant to be simple. I have been inspired by Christ's words during the trying periods of my life. I have found comfort from reading the scriptures.

One can find a beginning within life by viewing life as a whole rather than in small parts. It is, of course, how we live every moment that matters, and it is what we do that justifies our stay here on earth. But when we view life as a whole, anything can be for us at the beginning of, or at the end of some part of the big picture; it all depends on our outlook.

I will always try to surround myself with warm and expressive souls who go through life with courage and determination; that is: people who tend to overcome obstacles. I prefer to follow those who know that they can change their course in life, no matter how the road winds around, no matter how long it takes; I prefer to follow those who strive to reach their full potential.

Marian "Pat" Benedict Cmdr. USN NC Ret.

The Silence of the Pain is Deafening

My childhood and my inharmonious upbringing were conditions and hurdles I had to overcome if I ever wanted to see a broader vision of my life. The divorce of my parents was buried in my mind, crippling me with pain for many years until I found a place to put this extra load of loathsome baggage. I put my pain and confusion in the hands of God. The divorce, my parents' rage and sadness crippled me. So I prayed to change my feelings about the past. And finally, after what seemed a million years, I blew away the old file of anger and ugliness, so that I might become the person whom God intended for me to be. Only God can look into my soul and know my thoughts and potential; only God can pull out the darkness within me and snuff it out permanently. Some psychiatrists and psychologists believe they can look into our psyches or define our deliberations. However, they really don't know what we think unless we verbalize it. Their work, faulty and fallible, is entirely dependent upon our ability to accurately verbalize. God has no such limitations. God simply knows.

It has taken years for me to learn that I owe respect to my inner thoughts and feelings; that is: enough respect to share them with others. When I share my inner feelings, I also give my love freely to those around me. That way I can be a channel for ideas, questions, logic, arguments and philosophies. When

My Story

Forward

we give ourselves to others like that, we should give freely and unconditionally. Conditional gifts are really not gifts at all, and conditions prevent us from being a ray of sunshine in someone's life.

I believe that reading the spiritual works of God can help any of us to minimize our overwhelming pride and ego. Prayers, sacrifices and self-discipline have been my passion, and they differentiate me from many other people. These patterns of devotion can be flexible and ever-changing; so that any of us can indulge in them.

Blessed is the individual who recognizes and accepts the special people whom God places in his or her path. I have found there is nothing greater and nobler than a friend, and I believe that the meaning behind friendship is that it always provides returns, one way or another.

Although I love people– whomever they may be– God and my inner sanctity come first. On board a jet or airplane, the flight attendants tell parents with children to first apply the air masks to themselves in order to able to save their children. Similarly, it makes sense that, if we are to be of service to others, we must be stable and in good condition ourselves. I believe that my ability to work with people stems from my ability to see God within everything. I do not separate my

Marian "Pat" Benedict Cmdr. USN NC Ret.

spirituality from any moment in my life. I believe that we all have the ability to own the qualities of Christ-consciousness.

Since I was very young I have had a spiritual relationship with the Master. If I did not have this bond, then my heart and my life would cease to exist. Not only does He exist in human beings, He is in all creatures, plants and inanimate objects. God is every breath I take in, it is God who helps me exhale. It is not humanly possible to think of God every single minute. But I try to keep my focus on spiritual thoughts and positive ideas because it allows heaven to exist as part of my earthly world. It seems that I have searched my whole life for the Creator and, until the past few years, I did not pay attention to the Presence as much as I do now. I now know that god is always next to me, walking the steps I walk, and holding my hand when I grow weary and my eyes grow dim.

When I contemplate God and pray to be a channel and distributor of god's power, I want the spiritual force to rush through my body and mind, and so I demand discipline within myself. There are times when I do not connect and feel enthusiastic and satisfied from my prayers. I sometimes fear that I am not worthy of a close spiritual relationship with God. This sort of fear is a great enemy of mankind. The fear of not being good enough to learn the spiritual path comes from a lack of confidence in oneself. Such fear can get in the way of

Forward

true devotion and keeps a person from being lifted up by God's grace. Most of my life I have lived with fear, anger, greed, lust and vanity. All of these negative emotions are attached to the physical world's emphasis on materialism. These materialistic passions were my prison.

I was also a people-pleaser, putting my needs second to the wants of those around me. Alcohol allowed me to abandon my needs and replace self-interest with self-abuse. It took seventeen years of sobriety before I became comfortable with taking care of me. I searched for ways to accept myself and re-channel my self- loathing with self-love and self-acceptance. I wanted to accept all of my feelings and emotions. In order to do this I had to nurture the child within.

I helped myself to understand that I am but one human creature in a vast world of life. I knew that I could be more than I had been if I allowed God to be my light within. The influence of society, the collective sense of what modern culture thinks should be right and wrong, can make people think they themselves are God. But I don't believe that we should take God's place in that way, nor do I think that people can be one with God. I do believe that I can be a co-worker with God, keeping in mind the words of God and holding to the path lit by His eternal light.

Marian "Pat" Benedict Cmdr. USN NC Ret.

The Silence of the Pain is Deafening

Love leads the way: not the human love, but divine love. These two kinds of love, human and divine, are different; they pull us in opposite directions. Sometimes we think that, when we experience human love, we are experiencing divine love. However, the human and divine aspects of love are distinctly different.

I have often found myself divided between the selfish desire to be physically loved, and the need for divine love. Fearing, on the one hand, loneliness and endless desire; feeling, on the other hand, that I cannot have divine love unless I purify my yearnings for physical pleasure. I realize that I could have been an extremist, totally devoting myself to God, living like a nun and excluding myself from everyday life. But I always believed in balancing physical love and divine love. Had I so separated myself from life, I would not have gone through many of my learning experiences, and my spiritual growth would have been greatly impaired.

I look forward to the day when lasting solutions to many of our most profound problems are found through human understanding and compassion. Human power and exploitation condemn our societies to violence, misery and anxiety. My faith in human compassion, faith like a young child's hope, beautifies my picture of the entire world. This

Forward

confidence I have in human nature, is like the confidence we have in each day's sunlight.

Anyone, anywhere, at any time can work for and attain whatever God has chosen for that person to attain in this life. Although God's will may be at times hidden and not fully understood, it will come about for those who surrender to Him. God's will comes about, but often times: not without tears.

We are, only because God Is. Whoever we are, whatever we are, wherever we are there is no denying that or proving otherwise. This book is about people. Where they have been, where they are now, and importantly: where they are going. Because there is one certainty: we are all going home. Each life, be it short or long, is spent going home. That's what life is, since there is no other place to go. Home is the destination of each soul. It is a pity that some of us never realize why we are, or what our purpose is; but really, life is just a journey home. While for some, life is not worth living, every life is worthwhile in God's eyes, or it would not have been created.

Some people never get that we have a debt to God; others go through life knowing that we owe ourselves to God. Still others may know this intellectually, but it doesn't reach their inner selves. We belong completely and entirely to God; this is the reason for life.

Marian "Pat" Benedict Cmdr. USN NC Ret.

The Silence of the Pain is Deafening

I write this book not knowing who, if anyone, will read it. But my primary reason for writing is not to communicate with other people; other people are my secondary audience. I write because I feel a great need, from somewhere deep inside, to tell my Master that He alone is all. And I wish to tell Him through means other than Prayer.

My life story begins at a time before time. From before the beginning, I was in the mind of God. To write about myself alone would be entirely incorrect. Because myself, like every created being, always was. That is to say that all life has always existed in the mind of God. So I write of my life in light of God, with Him in mind, and indeed: to Him.

It is not the people in my life who should answer for where I've been and what I've done; it is I who must answer for my life. I am the one who was born alone and who will die alone. When I was at my best, I knew the triumph of high achievement. When at my worst, I failed and knew defeat. Looking back now, I find comfort in knowing that when I failed, I failed while trying. Those who have had victories in their lives, also know defeat. So, looking back on my failures, I know that my place is not with those cold and timid souls who know neither victory nor defeat.

I cannot fully penetrate other people when describing my love affair with God, because only God can see into my soul

Forward

and know what is there. It has taken me 43 years of sobriety to fully learn the respect I owe to Him. Help comes from God in return for prayers and sacrifice. I always knew this, but it took a long time for me to accept it.

There are those who pass through our lives only briefly, but in a way, the people who enter our lives are each a helping hand to heaven. Blessed is the individual who recognizes the special person whom God has placed in his path. When two friends are together, of one heart and mind, in the House of God, they can see Christ in one another, and that becomes a source of love.

I know that I have never been without Him. If it were otherwise, my physical heart would have stopped. He is all things. It is God who causes my every breath. We cannot think of Him constantly, for even if we were able to do so during our awakened hours, He is not present in our minds throughout our sleep. And yet, if He forgot us for an instant we would no longer be.

Throughout my life I have looked for Him, although until the last few years, I have been unaware of looking for Him much of the time. I went for long periods unaware that He walks with me. He is a mystery to me; a mystery, yet all knowing. During my prayers, if I do not feel that satisfaction and enthusiasm from my interaction with God, then I won't

Marian "Pat" Benedict Cmdr. USN NC Ret.

have it within myself after my prayers. The greatest hurdle to a strong relationship with God is self-confidence derived from other sources. Turning to sources other than God for confidence and strength is a root of failure.

I dedicate this book to God because without this source I know that I would not exist. Even though we are not equal in this human realm, we are all equal in the sight of God. We are all moving in the same direction: home to the heavenly spheres. All of our lives, short or long, are spent trying to discover the source from whence we came; our home. While home may be a cloudy concept in our mind's eye, our souls, as pure souls, know what home truly means.

When my Master calls, I know that I will be free and unafraid of leaving my body and this world as I know it. Someone may say, "Oh look at that poor soul on the street, begging for a scrap of bread." I do not pity that human being nor worry that he may have wasted his life. I know that the 'bums' and the 'drunks' are their own unique people. Existence is God's greatest gift. Nothing is more wonderful than being, than just plain existing, whether in this world or in the next.

My Story

Chapter One
The Early Years

The Early Years

I was born into a very dysfunctional home. I absolutely hated it. As a child, my ill feelings towards my home were so intense that I would silently scream at the walls in my room.

Mistrust

I was raised by several different people; not solely by my mother and father. This exposure to different influences, which yielded mixed and inconsistent messages, resulted in mistrust. At a very early age, I learned to suppress most of my feelings, because the world of grownups was not trustworthy. I could not trust in the conflicting information I received, so I trusted in my own answers to my searching questions. I did not ask grownups about sex, death, love or other deep subjects, so my intense probing into the depths of reality found answers only from within my immature mind. Sometimes I was too embarrassed to ask; other times I felt that the grownups in my life were not worthy to answer me; but inconsistent responses from the various grownups was the main cause of my turning within myself, suppressing my feelings and trying to define my own reality.

Abandonment

When I was three years old, during the great depression, my father took off; he left us. I grew up in a household of dysfunctional relationships, poverty and chaos. I don't recall anyone ever seriously listening to me as a youngster. I was not close to anyone during my childhood, with the exception of a strong relationship with my cousin Bob. Later in my life I formed a close relationship with my sister Jane, but as a child, I felt misunderstood and alienated from other people in my family, and even from my childhood friends.

As a child I fluctuated between loving the world and hating the world. There was an emptiness, a hole inside of me, a hole which, to this day, I have not been able to fill. I could not stop that overwhelming, aching feeling of abandonment.

Dysfunctional Mother

My mother was not there for me during my early childhood. Later I realized that my mother was playing victim. I still don't really understand the source of that selfishness which was in her. She was complicated; she may have been manic-depressive. My mother's various drug prescriptions included tranquilizers and mood altering drugs. Looking back I can't be certain if the drugs caused her mood swings or if she took them because of her mood swings. I am still sad that she could not have given herself to me with purity and simplicity. My mother had a controlling

> **Excursus:**
> **The Effects of a Difficult Childhood on Drinking and Sobriety**
> Following my transition from drinking to sobriety, I underwent group therapy. One day when I was sitting in group therapy, our therapist Dr. Rader asked me: "How are you feeling?" I did not answer because I could not relate to the question. I felt like my life was a piece of shit. I felt that my experiences in Vietnam had done some damage to me. However, as a child, to protect myself, I had learned to shut down my feelings, emotions and my thoughts and to send them out into orbit. This protective behavior pattern left me incapable of saying "I am angry" or "I am devastated" or "I am

nature, which was difficult for me, but it was my unfulfilled desire to interact with my mother that I found so painful.

I cannot recall my mother ever reaching out her arms to hug or kiss me. I would walk in the door and reach out to her with open arms; she never would approach me. I was the one who was always reaching for her love, while her affection was contingent. What affection she showed me was contingent upon her mood and upon whether or not she thought I was a good enough little girl. I adjusted to her coldness, but I still cannot explain it. Simply stated, our household was not a warm, understanding or compassionate environment. We did have times of laughter and fun, and physical abuse was minimal (other than

feeling abused."
Dr. Rader pointed out to me that I should allow myself to experience real feelings. By 'real' he meant my personal feelings as they applied to me. By getting in touch with my own feelings, I was able to experience a greater sense of wholeness and of being in touch, first with myself, and then with other people.

Group Benefits
It was in group therapy that I experienced internal revelations about some of the traumas I had been through. I realized that, there in group therapy, there were people who could genuinely empathize with me and comfort me. The people in therapy and I were seeking to become self-realized and healed by

frequent spankings), but our home was emotionally vacant. There was no openness; there was no real, sincere kindness.

Hatred

While I was emotionally abused by my mother through her coldness and neglect, it was my father whom I hated, even though he was not around. Until recently, I would be overcome with feelings of rage and hatred whenever anyone mentioned my father. I carried this hate campaign around with me until a peer from Alcoholics Anonymous asked me, "How in the name of God can you hate someone you don't even know?"

I had no answer to that question. I was stunned by my own inability to respond, and I looked within myself. It was like I had stepped off a torturous rocky side of a mountain and was now looking at the

> developing a better understanding of human nature through one another.
> When I would hear the same poignant message coming from different people, a message which would strike a nerve, then I would look within myself to see if what I heard corresponded to what was there. The messages I received in this manner definitely meant something. They were telling me to open up my ego-centered mind and to listen to other people's comprehension of my behavior. People who wish to inform others about their perceptions of them should be unattached and non-judgmental. The saying we use at Alcoholics Anonymous concerning this is "Live

Marian "Pat" Benedict Cmdr. USN NC Ret.

whole mountain from afar. Looking at the whole picture and taking into account the flaws of human nature, I washed away the hate, self-pity and negativity from my repertoire of emotions for my father. I realized that I was the one suffering from the ugliness of hatred; at the same time I realized that no one should hate. When you hate it's like hating yourself. The other person cannot feel your hatred. Instead, you are the only one who can feel this ugly emotion.

Love and Hatred for a Manipulative Victim

My mother was often sick, or so it seemed. I remember her having sinus headaches every weekend. Later I figured out that she was a manipulator. My sister Jane and I would put hot packs on her head every Saturday and Sunday so that we could

> and Let Live."
> I wanted to scream as a child, and to tell my family to go to hell, but I never could verbalize my feelings. A lot of bitterness and anger kept getting buried deeper inside of me. I became an expert at bulldozing all the hurt I felt deep down inside of me. Instead of verbalizing and communicating, I screamed silently to my bedroom walls.
> I am sure that the day I found alcohol was the day that I was first able to release some of these horrible, haunting hurts into the outside world. Some people get into emotional relationships to deal with life. Some people become "workaholics." Some people take "uppers" to

The Early Years

soothe her pain. It would stop her from complaining, so we didn't mind taking the trouble. When I was about thirteen and experiencing my own menstrual pain, I had to care for myself. I realized then that my mother had used me and would never care for me the way she got me to care for her.

My mother was able to control me to a large extent by being conveniently sick. For instance, I could not play with my friends on many weekends because my mother would require constant attention. I think she did that because she couldn't stand to be alone with her thoughts. It was hard to turn away from my mother. I hated her and resented her demands, but at the same time, because I saw her weakness, I also loved her and gave myself freely. I have seen this sort of

> run away from life. Some people take "downers" to drown out life. Then there are those who get drunk. Often we wind up unloading our stored up misery on some undeserving soul.
>
> ### God Understands
> Through all of my misery, however, God could always see what I was about. Knowing that God was watching and fully aware of me helped me to survive. There are forces greater than us; forces that can swish into our lives, pick up our drenched souls and renew our spirit's glow. We should always be open to this kind of energy and rejuvenation, and we are opened through our beliefs. The rejuvenated person will then be able to experience life with a

Marian "Pat" Benedict Cmdr. USN NC Ret.

love-hate relationship affecting the lives of other parents and children. From my own experience, I became more sensitive and understanding about this sort of duality in others.

whole new attitude. There were brief moments of being comfortable with myself when I would put my attention on the source. I knew deep down that I was understood and accepted for who I was. God was the only one who knew what I was really going through. The pain, anger, anxiety, frustration and the insecurities that many of us walk around with, may never be shared with any other human being. But God always knows, and He can be a great comfort throughout life.

Self-acceptance: Comfort amid Pain

As an alcoholic, I found it difficult to say what was on my mind. Instead, I would joke about things that were affecting me. I wouldn't put myself on

The Soul Chooses

My mother suffered most of her life, but she steered her life in the direction of difficulties. She divorced my father and had to raise two children on her own. I sometimes resented her for bringing me into a world of misery and pain. I wanted to ask her why she would bring two children into her joyless life. Deep down inside, I blamed her for being so inconsiderate as to give me life. I realize now that it was not her fault that I am here on earth. I now understand that we come into this world of our own volition and inspiration. My birth had nothing to do with my parents having

The Early Years

sexual intercourse. I believe that as a soul I chose to enter life in order to fulfill my need to learn and grow.

Socially Withdrawn Mother and Daughter

My mother was so reclusive and depressed that many people thought she was a widow. She was actually a widow only at the end of her life, since my father died before she did. But she might as well have been a widow during her lifetime, since he wasn't around. I felt embarrassed and inadequate being fatherless; I compensated by being a people-pleaser. My life was characterized by the need to please others.

Other behavior patterns which grew out of my growing up in a broken, fatherless home involved withdrawing from other people. When people tried to be kind to me, I would

the line in case someone would negate my feelings. Out of all the feelings I can remember, the feeling of not really caring about anything at all is the most prevalent. "I'm not interested." Or: "I don't really want to get involved" or: "I don't give a shit" were often my attitudes. I had these feelings for years, all through my nursing career and in the military. I carried this attitude with me, first to Africa and then to Vietnam. The feeling of empty pain pervaded my being, and the silence of this pain was deafening.

One day in Vietnam I was sitting on my bed after cleaning up a young Vietnamese soldier and there was a loud ringing in my ears. Then all of sudden everything became

The Silence of the Pain is Deafening

shy away. I could not handle attention or compliments. I would hide away from any kind of genuine love and caring. When surrounded by functional people, I wanted to just blend into the walls and disappear for fear they would notice something different about me. Often I didn't want people to talk to me or even look at me.

Poverty of Nurturing Love
Paucity of Self-confidence

My mother always managed to have food on the table for my sister Jane and me. We always had clothes to wear –I wore hand-me-downs on through high school– our mother taught us that we must be grateful for the used clothing and reminded us constantly of how good it was of others to give to our poor family.

> really quiet. I couldn't hear any sound at all, but I realized that I was clutching my hands over my ears. It was then that I understood that the suppression of my feelings was making me cold and insensitive. My head felt like it all was mixed up inside. I really didn't know what I was all about. I couldn't know myself or understand my feelings because I had learned to suppress them as a child. This was because my feelings weren't accepted, as I was not accepted. And it was at that moment that I realized that I did not accept myself.
> I have been in a constant struggle to achieve the positive traits I admire. When I was drinking and

The Early Years

I had rarely experienced outward love from my mother. I knew from observing my friends' families in action that I was missing out on the positive, 'warm and fuzzy' feelings life can offer. This lack of nurturing love left me unable to trust others. I was suspicious of everyone I knew, and I was uncomfortable with myself. I felt weird, as if my clothes were inappropriate, as if I didn't belong with others. Later in life, as a Navy Commander, I was still not able to feel proud or happy with myself. Even today, when I walk into a room or go onstage to speak, I feel self-conscious and terrified of making a mistake.

> people would ask, "What are you looking for?" my answer would be "Relief." If someone asked me that question today, I would say, "Peace," meaning peace within myself. The only thing I really needed to find tranquility within was the ability to accept myself. The people around me and rest of the world were not the cause of the miserable state I was in. I needed to take responsibility for getting to know myself, and then accepting myself and picking myself back up. For me to accept my own self, I needed to take inventory of all my failures, my accomplishments, my positive and negative characteristics, and my sins. I almost had to make an appointment with myself in order to

Tomboy

There is much emphasis on appearance in our society, and it was in that shallow arena that my feelings of inadequacy developed. I was overly conscientious of my appearance and concerned with how others observed me. I now realize that such self-consciousness is a character defect. As a child I was uncomfortable with my body, with its mystery and all its imperfections. Being female in our society can create disturbing inhibitions and disgust for the human body. I decided that society liked males better, so I became a tomboy. It was not just that I felt that our society put girls second; I really felt that I should have been a boy. I was so self-conscious of this that I began to contemplate suicide at an early age. I didn't share these feelings with anyone at the time.

My family was displeased with my behavior as a child. I was harassed and I felt humiliated at family gatherings; I was picked on and scapegoated, and that was painful for me to endure.

> bring myself to a sense of reality. I heard a saying in AA: "When you stop digging, you'll find out more about yourself." I thought that was a profound statement because it took a lot for me to finally stop digging. It's just like telling a dog to stop digging; it is such a natural thing for us to delve and shovel our shit. I went through phases, ups and downs, Christianity and no Christianity, and I was forever shutting out my emotions. It was a continuous struggle, but finally, at last, I became comfortable with "me."

The Early Years

As a child I was full of love, high energy and lust for life. Maybe it was because these were precisely the qualities that my family's philosophies opposed that I suffered so much negative energy. Maybe they were trying to channel my daring nature into more passive and acceptable behavior; behavior more consistent with their ideas of a girl.

I still feel the repercussions of the persecutions I suffered as a child. It wasn't until after I turned 60 that I realized that I am a creative individual in a society of non-caring, inconsiderate, self-centered robots. That realization freed me from other people's imposed restrictions. These days I really don't give a shit whether I'm liked or disliked, because I feel love for myself, and I am able to feel at least an impersonal love for the people around me, whatever they may think.

Addiction to Emotions

My sister Jane and I were raised in a very strict environment. We were punished often, while my aunts and uncles were more lenient with my cousins. I think my mother mistreated us to prove to other people that she was in control of us. On one occasion the grownups in my family had gone to the cemetery to pay respects to family members who had passed on. Locked out, my sister Jane and I, and our cousins all crawled in through Aunt Lena's window to get something to eat. All of us had crawled through that window, yet only my sister and I were punished for it. We were taken behind the shed, screamed at and whipped. I came back into Aunt Lena's house after the whipping was over and washed the tears from my face. I felt completely humiliated and I tried to cover up my discomfort and shame. My mother was not so much angry that we crawled through the window; rather, she was embarrassed. Embarrassed that our misbehavior made her seem inadequate. So my mother made Jane and me sit on chairs in front of our relatives so she could boast in our regret. I sat there trying to pull the hem of my dress down around my ankles to hide the stripes on my legs where I had been whipped.

Once when I was at the dinner table I asked my sister to pass the gravy. We were all there: my mom, my aunt Bobby, her son, cousin Bob, and my sister Jane.

Well, Jane either didn't hear me or she was ignoring me, so I spoke up: "Hand me the Goddamn gravy!"

She did, and my mother waited while I put some on my mashed potatoes. Then she slapped me across the face hard enough to knock me to the floor.

Everyone else at the table just continued to eat while my mother spoke slowly: "You will never use the Lord's Name that way in this house again. You will get up, not pout, finish your dinner and you, Bob and Jane will clean everything up and do the dishes."

Then, of course, Bob and Jane were angry at me as well.

This strict upbringing later enhanced my addiction to alcohol; specifically, a type of addiction was added to my alcoholism: an addiction to emotions. When a person grows up governed by control and constraint, implemented by corporal punishment, as a child the person becomes accustomed to imposed control and fails to develop self-control. As an adult, the person then indulges in negative emotions as a familiar means toward self-control. The person becomes dependent upon negative emotions to function properly, and this dependency has the characteristics of addiction.

Escape and People Pleasing

Jane escaped from our difficult home by getting married young. She moved on from a painful childhood by leading her own life at an early age. I also fled our restrictive home by attending nursing school as a live-in student. But then I joined the military where I found myself still trying to please people just as I had with my mother. I think my pattern of trying please others was one of the things that kept me in nursing as a profession. I believe that underlying the reasons why people work as nurses is that many of us are nurturers; that is: people who seek approval by giving to others. I was seeking admiration. I assumed people would think of me as a Florence Nightingale type, and I thought that would be cool. But also: being a nurse was emotionally rewarding.

Buying Love, Appreciation and Acceptance

It was easy for me to think that the way to receive love was to buy it or trade for it. I was always trying to buy people's love, understanding and appreciation. For some reason I had to continue with this humiliating behavior for many years before I realized how easy it was for people to take advantage of me. Today, because of my sobriety and elevated self-esteem, my emotional needs are easier to meet. I now see that in the past I was always seeking approval. I don't think that most of the people I became involved with truly cared about me; rather, they had expectations of me. They expected me to perform for them, and so I assumed the roles they set forth for me.

The older I became the more I suppressed my feelings, the more I backed away from confrontation and the more I hid my needs. Eventually, I was managing my life by shoving all my pain and loneliness into the pockets of my mind. I was also becoming angry inside, wanting to crawl out from under my self-imposed repressions.

The Early Years

I was not successful in achieving personal independence until I stopped drinking alcohol. The professional help I got during the initial recovery from alcoholism included therapies, and so, for the first time in my life, I started to be honest with myself about my feelings. Dealing honestly with my feelings was very hard to do. I looked back at my life and tried to rationalize. I asked myself whether my problems were my own responsibility or were they linked to the way my mother treated me.

I am sure my mother loved me in some way, however I don't remember even once that she ever said so; not to me nor to my sister. I believe she did love me as a mother loves a daughter, that is: she felt a kind of love born of maternal instincts. But I don't think that she loved me or even liked me as a person, and this led to my feeling of not being likeable. As this feeling that I was not a likeable person surfaced, I started to strive for internal independence.

It took years of soul-searching, and winding up in some pretty bad situations, before I felt worthy of good, sober, sound company. I found out as I matured in sobriety that I did not have to be accepted by a lot of people to feel good about myself. I can be close to a few people, and have an impersonal love for the rest of the lot. I have respect, compassion and

Marian "Pat" Benedict Cmdr. USN NC Ret.

understanding for every individual that I meet; however, I won't always like everyone I meet.

Having the option to care or to not care about whether one is accepted by others can make one feel a hell of a lot more comfortable.

My Story

Chapter Two
Childhood

The Silence of the Pain is Deafening

When I was seven my cousin Bob and his mother, my mother's sister Bobbie, moved in with us (or we moved in with them- whichever it was). It was a time in my life and in my sister Jane's life when we tried to have some fun. Cousin Bob was a fun guy. My memories of that portion of my life are a bit blurred, but I can bring back good feelings when I think about me and Bob living under the same roof. Money for any recreational activity was limited, so we made up a lot of our own fun. We were able to make fun out of anything, or out of nothing at all.

I remember life in that household being characterized by our daily routines. We did chores every Friday evening. These included laundry, vacuuming, dusting and finishing the homework that was due the following week. When my sister, Bob and I finished our chores, we had Saturday and Sunday to play—that is, we could play if mom wasn't too sick.

Naughty Fun

The biggest thing we did on Saturdays was to walk to the Villa Theatre which was three or four blocks from our house. We would go through an underpass at Cleveland Elementary School, rather than try to cross 23rd Street. It wasn't really that far, but we played along the way and we had small bladders. There were places where we could pee: in the bushes along the way, or in the underpass. Jane and I would be on the lookout while Bob would relieve himself. Then he would watch out for us while we went. These episodes were really fun times for us. All we were doing was peeing in public, but it was such a challenge not to get caught that we were all giggles.

Fun at the Theater

At the Villa Theater we always sat in the seats to the right, by the first light on the wall. I don't know how that routine came about, but that was where bob and my sister and I could be found every time. When my older cousin Gordon would join us at the theater, he would know where to find us since we never failed to sit in our special seats. From time to time Gordon would sneak up and scare us, causing us to jolt and scream like fools.

We went to the Villa, not only to see the featured film, but to see the continuation of a regular series that was going on for some time. The series was Zorro, and it ended with a cliffhanger, week after week. The cost to get in was dime. We never had the money to buy popcorn or candy or coke; at least I don't remember ever being able to do so. I'm sure that is one reason why I now buy popcorn every time I go to the movies.

I'm sure Aunt Bobbie and my mom were relieved to have some time without us. They probably went to the grocery store, washed their hair, fixed their nails or took care of some of the chores before heading back to work on Monday morning. These recollections of family life are among the happier ones of my childhood. I wish they were more representative of my childhood as a whole.

An Aunt and Uncle Nearby

One of my mother's older sisters was Aunt Fay. She and her husband Uncle Vern were two other people who raised me. Aunt Fay, Uncle Vern and my cousins Garnet and Gordon lived just three houses up from us. I didn't have much to do with Garnet since she was much older. However, there was a time when I seemed to idolize my cousin Gordon who was just a few years older than me. I remember Gordon in his garage with stacks and stacks of comic books; so many that you could literally wade through them. Somehow, though he tried to pile them into stacks, they always wound up all over the floor of the garage. They were everywhere. My cousin Bob and I worked for Gordon when he sold "reading time" to neighborhood kids. Gordon would hang the comic books on coat hangers and the neighborhood children would come by to read them. Gordon would charge them a small amount so the kids wouldn't have to buy the comic books; they could just rent them for a time. Gordon charged them according to how popular the comic book was—it cost one penny or two pennies to sit and read one. I would sweep out the garage once in a while to keep busy. I would only clean while listening to an

Childhood

old crank-style Victrola Gramophone which I would wind up and play. I'd put records on and collect the money for Gordon after the kids finished reading. Gordon never paid any of us for helping him out, but that was what occupied our time during the summer while our mothers were at work.

Granny Left an Impression

During this time a woman came to live with us and take care of us. We called her "granny." I can't remember her real name. Maybe I never knew it; she was always just granny to us. I think my mother paid her $5 a month. Granny had room and board, and she took care of my cousin Bob, Jane and I when our parents worked. She had long hair that was braided and she had no teeth. We adored and loved her to pieces, but we would also get mad at her. In fact, I fired her on several occasions. I would fire her and she would just look at me. I was just a child, but she would feel completely intimidated and upset by my actions. I remember vividly that she had a real crush on a famous movie star, Robert Taylor. Her adoration of Robert Taylor was to the point of an obsession. Granny took care of us for several years. I don't remember exactly when she left, but the impression of her warmth and caring remains tucked away in my mind.

In our small home on 21st Street I slept with my mother, and Bob and his mother slept in twin beds in a separate room.

Marian "Pat" Benedict Cmdr. USN NC Ret.

The Silence of the Pain is Deafening

A back bedroom was added on to the house at about that time, and my sister Jane slept there with granny. We didn't have electric blankets in those days, and it was freezing at night, so in the winter Mom would heat a brick and wrap it in a lose blanket, then place it at our feet.

My cousin Gordon had a paper route. I would go with him in the evening and help him. We would ride double on his bicycle and I would go with him to help him collect money from his paper delivery route. The Sunday papers were very thick, so my Uncle Vern would help Gordon deliver them. They would load them in the car and Gordon would throw them out the window as Uncle Vern drove by.

Small Community Suffers Loss

Like a puppy dog, I followed Gordon and his best friend, Gene Lilly, everywhere they went. Gene lived over on the next block. He was the same age as my sister Jane and my cousin Gordon, and I looked up to him as an older, wiser person. He joined the Marines and was killed in Korea. This was very traumatic for me, and it was a severe blow to his parents. Gene's mother was so stricken with the news of her son's death that her life came to a halt. She remained in the same house that Gene grew up in until her own death, and I am sure she never stopped mourning the death of her son. We were first officially notified of Gene's death, and then an article with his picture appeared in the newspaper. It was a horrible experience for me. I was deeply saddened, as were all of us in the community. Even today when Gordon and I talk on the phone, Gene's name will come up.

Let's You Kids Go to Church

My mother and Aunt Bobbie were very insistent that my sister Jane, my cousin Bob and I must all attend Sunday school and church with Aunt Fay, Uncle Vern and our cousins, Gordon and Garnet. Aunt Fay taught Sunday school and we were in her class. During the summer months when Aunt Fay taught Vacation Bible School, we also were required to attend, even though it was our summer vacation. Neither my mother nor my Aunt Bobbie attended church, but probably sent us to try to keep us out of trouble. We had to memorize Psalms and other parts of the Bible. If we memorized them properly, we would receive a ribbon that Aunt Fay made for all of us in our Sunday school class. We also received cutouts of stars or other symbols of Christianity as a reward. When I did well and got a gold star or ribbon, I felt very proud. The Psalms didn't mean anything to me but knowing I was able to memorize them made me happy. My Aunt Fay, whom I nicknamed Fayfee, was very proud of our memorizations, so everyone at Sunday school was happy, despite the fact that we did not learn the meaning of the Bible texts.

Marian "Pat" Benedict Cmdr. USN NC Ret.

The Silence of the Pain is Deafening

My mother never complemented me on my ability to recite parts of the Bible, nor did she show any interest in Bible study. She never seemed to take pride or experience any satisfaction from my religious education. Mother and Aunt Bobbie had little interest in church, but they expected us to attend. This didn't bother me because I enjoyed the various activities the church offered.

One time I played a shepherd boy in the Christmas pageant at the evangelical church. I got the part because none of the boys wanted it. Several of us dressed up as shepherds and stood at the crib of the Christ child during this Christmas pageant. My mother attended the pageant one Saturday or Sunday evening. I remember wanting to be a part of the Christmas festivities and feeling proud of my part in the Christmas play. I did not feel special because I was chosen as a shepherd because everybody was assigned one part or another. But I felt special just to be a part of the group. I loved being depended upon and wanted by others, and I enjoyed being responsible to people who appreciated my efforts.

Early Work Responsibility

My sister, my cousin Bob and I were expected to work for and earn our own spending money. The first job I ever had was baby-sitting at ten cents an hour. It didn't matter how many kids someone had, the pay was still ten cents an hour. My

Childhood

cousin Bob lived in California for a short period of time. His first job was at the bowling alley there, near his California house. Later, when bob and his mom moved in with us, he had a job at Bile's nursery, where he made ten cents an hour working for old man Bile, whom we nicknamed B.B.B.B.B., which stood for Baby Boy Bilious Bad Bile.

Corporate Entrepreneurs

In order to have as much spending money as possible, Bob and I became very business-minded when we were still very young. I don't remember how old Bob and I were when we decided to start an insurance company to protect everyone's assets. We made a go of it with some free home resources: a cigar box, a little notebook, as well as note-pads and lots of white and colored scrap paper my mother brought home from the Oklahoma Paper Company, where she worked. The company would throw out fragments of paper, which we recycled. We used them for our insurance company, and also for other things like Valentine's Day cards. I don't recall ever buying a Valentine's Day card; instead we made our own beautiful and unique cards. It was a wonderful experience; we could not afford to purchase cards, and we were grateful just to have the pieces of paper to make ours out of. We even made our own glue; it was granny who taught us how to mix flour and water to make paste.

Marian "Pat" Benedict Cmdr. USN NC Ret.

The Silence of the Pain is Deafening

So Bob and I got innovative and founded our insurance company. It took some planning, but we devised a way to protect our families' welfare and prized possessions. We charged everybody in the house five cents to be insured in case they were injured in the house or in case anything of theirs was missing or destroyed. We charged my sister Jane only three cents because she didn't have any money, and because she had very few items to insure. I explained to Jane that eventually our insurance company would be a large corporation, but she was not too thrilled about the whole endeavor. As it turned out our insurance company lasted only about two months, and then

we just dissolved it, pocketed our profits and everyone forgot about it. Everyone, that is, except Bob and I. Bob pocketed most of the money, and he still owes me about twenty or thirty cents.

My Story

Childhood

Bob and I worried over every little dime in those days. The money and material things we had, and the movies we were able to see, gave Bob and me a feeling of self-worth. We were out to earn a buck and we would make money any way we could. Because we valued every cent we earned, we did not spend our money foolishly, but saved it. If we wanted something badly enough, we saved up and bought it.

Early Employment

My first real job required a work permit, since I was only twelve years old. My mother helped me to land a summer job working at Oklahoma Paper Company. My job, filing various charts, paid minimal wages, as did most jobs in those days. I had a chance to work with my cousin Garnet, who worked at the switchboard, and eventually, I learned enough to fill in on the switchboard at noon. Another cousin, Nellie, who lived in the country, came to live with Aunt Fay and Uncle Vern. Since she worked at Equitable Life Insurance, which was near the paper company, she carpooled with my mother, Garnet and me to work.

Cousin Gordon

My cousin Gordon lived just a few houses down the street from where my mom and Aunt Bobbie, my sister Jane, my cousin Bob and myself all lived. Gordon was like an older brother, or sometimes like a father to me. We would work together, building model airplanes and kites. We designed our own paper kites using newspaper, sticks and glue.

Christmas Prank

Christmas was only as fun as we made it in those days. We would usually receive a minimal amount of gifts. We didn't have money to buy fancy bulbs and ornaments, so we made most of our own decorations for the tree and the house. There was one Christmas when our mothers insisted that we fix up the tree, but neither Bob, Jane nor I were in the mood to make Christmas stuff. So we made some funky stocking socks, and then we wrapped them individually like little gifts and strung them all through the Christmas tree. We laughed at our disfigured Christmas ornaments.

We were anxious for everyone to open their gifts on Christmas morning. Our parents were surprised when we told them to open the funky ornaments we had made. When they each took a disfigured ornament off the tree and opened it up, our parents found that in each funky stocking there was a small wrapped package. When they opened up the packages they were shocked, surprised; even horrified to find a cold, slimy hot dog. I still can't help but giggle when I recall the Christmas that we gave our parents each a hot dog as a gift. Someone might think we were being mean; we were really only mocking how poor we were, not having any money for fancy gifts, or even much money for moderately-priced practical gifts.

Young Truck Driver

Of course our families couldn't afford private driving lessons; nor, if our school had offered lessons, could we have afforded those. My cousin Gordon learned to drive at home in his dad's coffee truck. He would practice by driving up and down the driveway. When I was about ten, before we had moved in with them, my mother and I were visiting Aunt Fay. My mom asked about the noise coming from outside. My Aunt Fay told her that was Gordon, driving up and down the driveway, learning to shift gears. Just then it occurred to my mother that I was nowhere to be seen, so she went looking for me. She finally found me in the coffee truck, sitting on Gordon's lap. I was too small to sit in the driver's seat and work the steering wheel or the pedals, so Gordon was working the pedals and I was in his lap steering, while he was teaching me how to shift gears.

My mother freaked out and started yelling at Uncle Vern: "My God Vern, those kids are driving the coffee truck!"

He calmly said, "They have to learn to drive somewhere."

It was great for me when my older cousin Gordon would take the place of the father I didn't have, teaching me things like how to drive.

Marian "Pat" Benedict Cmdr. USN NC Ret.

The Silence of the Pain is Deafening

We didn't have much, so my cousins and I, along with our neighborhood friends, made our own fun. During this period we all learned how to play kick-the-can, and hide-and-go-seek. At night we would sit on blankets outside and tell ghost stories with the neighborhood kids. We used to get Jane to drive to pick up strawberry ice cream for us. But Jane got tired of strawberry ice cream. Eventually she grew to hate it, so she refused to get it for us anymore. We were smart enough to call the drug store and have the ice cream delivered. It didn't cost much more and we didn't have to compromise on our favorite flavor. Sometimes, in the summertime, we would all sleep outdoors on cots. In those days children could sleep in the open in safety. I think that when kids make their own fun they have the best fun.

Same Background, Different Personalities

Often, when I look back on my childhood, I think about my sister Jane. Sometimes it seems as though we were estranged as siblings. It isn't that we fought more than other kids, it was that we were different. My sister and I were opposites in our personalities and behavior. She was quiet and introspective; I was more of a tomboy, outgoing and extroverted. While Jane would play alone with her dolls in the house, I would be outside, playing ball or playing with rubber-band guns. While Jane was fitting into the mold of the ideal girl, I was

Childhood

developing into an individual; a nonconformist; a person whom, later on, I learned to take pride in being.

It wasn't until later in life that my sister Jane and I became very close. After I passed through my drinking phase and became sober, I began to understand a lot of things about her. The ways in which she and I were similar brought feelings of closeness to me, while I learned to appreciate her uniqueness in the ways in which we were different. I realized that my sister and I both learned to suppress our feelings and watch what we said at an early age. We both strove to please our mother and the harder we tried and failed, the more we had to withdraw inside ourselves. For both of us, this behavior pattern of suppression and withdrawal continued into adulthood, where it provided some common ground in our relationship.

Our Mother Edna

When I returned home from the navy, after the first two years, I asked my sister, "Why do you run around and try to please her?"

Marian "Pat" Benedict Cmdr. USN NC Ret.

Jane answered, "Because she's my mother," looking at me as if to say, "*You wouldn't understand.*"

Now I believe that I do understand. I think Jane never stopped looking for approval from our mother. I believe she wanted mother to hold her and say, "Hey, it's okay to make mistakes." Or, "It's okay to be wrong." It wasn't necessary for my sister to tolerate the pressure and fear my mother instilled in her for as long as she did. She maintained her own little prison; but all of us have, at times, wound webs around ourselves, and we all learn lessons at our own pace.

Edna, circa 1973

Whom to Please

I spent most of my childhood in a state of consternation, afraid that I was going to dissatisfy someone, and that fear caused me to become self-critical as well. It wasn't until later in life that I came to stop caring if my behavior met the criteria or desires of other people. Now I don't try to please anyone, because I know I can't please everyone. Jesus Christ did not appeal to everyone, so why should I think that I have the capacity to do so?

Suffering and Motherhood

I used to wonder if there was a real fulfilling love in my mother or a caring and devoted blissfulness she experienced with her children. I wondered: did my mother take pleasure from being a parent? In retrospect I don't think she did. I don't think she had her heart into the process to the extent necessary to be a gratified, nurturing mother. My mother seemed to feel poisoned and discontented because she had to raise two daughters in a world that was so unkind, a world in which such a woman would be impoverished without a man in her life. Because she had no husband around to help her, my mother became stifled and pathetically withdrawn; she lacked the sense of being a complete woman.

Act Normal; Don't Embarrass Me

Jane and I lived in fear of being an embarrassment to our mother. She always told us how to behave so that other people would think we were like everyone else. She wanted us to seem like two girls with a mom and dad, a nice house and a dog, even though we wore hand-me-downs until we were out on our own. Our mother wished to portray an image to hide the truth. I don't think she taught us behavior skills because

she loved us, or because she wanted us to feel adequate with other people. I believe she taught us these things because she did not want to risk her own embarrassment as a result of our conduct.

Jane and I were always in competition with our mother. We came first in a lot of things, in the way we wanted things to be, but mom always had the final say. She was in charge; she maintained control. By controlling my sister and me, she was able to feel in control of herself. I don't think that her particular demands really mattered to her. With our lives in the palm of her hand, she was able to feel self-assertive and masterful. In this way she gained the confidence to realize her own achievements in life.

Chapter Three
Recollections and Reflections

The Silence of the Pain is Deafening

Profitable Recollections

I now understand that I can ponder my childhood, my recollections of being poor, of having no father and of being raised by a bitter mother, and ponder them without a good result. Or I can ponder my past, my mother, my sister and my relationships with them in a way that helps accomplish a transformation within me. If I were to ponder the past without delving into the painful memories, without at least responding to my feelings, then I would have recollected my thoughts and past visions for nothing. I would have missed the insight into what my childhood was all about. To me, my past is a lesson on how to live in this world, and how to live in today.

Too Easy

I once resented, but now pity people who have had everything handed to them. I have seen adolescents who have never had to work for anything in their lives. Their parents provided for their every need, and they did so without expecting any particular level of performance from them. Having had everything provided for them left them incapable of managing their lives adequately. They tend to be immature; they tend to lack a sense of purpose and they lack the ability to appreciate the simpler things in life. A person who grows

My Story

up without the responsibility for achieving the gifts of life will become unmotivated and dull.

Accelerated Maturity: Benefit and Loss

I grew up sooner than I wanted to. I remember getting on a bus alone when I was eleven or twelve years old and taking it downtown. I was responsible to meet my mother at the bank; it was time to learn how to open a checking account. After I obtained my checks, we went to the gas company, the water company and the electric company. I was taught how to write checks and pay bills. Meanwhile, the other kids my age were out playing.

I know that I am better off for having been forced to be self-directed at an early age, yet sometimes I wish I had been a privileged child. I feel like I missed a good portion of my childhood, and that has left a void within me as an adult. Having grown up poor and grown up fast, I sometimes experience the natural child-like feelings of wanting to be pampered, of wanting everything done for me. I cope with these feelings by allowing the child within to surface, and then by loving this child with all of my heart. I struggle to regain the precious feelings of love from God that this child knew, the love that comforted this child's cry in the night.

As a child, I did not have to guess what was expected of me. Out of necessity, my mother trained my sister Jane and me to help her. She needed us to play the part of adults. She did not have the option of allowing us to be irresponsible. I believe that as a result I was more mature as a child. Later in life, as I began to drink alcohol, I seemed to become more childlike, as if I were experiencing a delayed childhood.

Dark and Rosy Memories

Now, as I walk back through my childhood memories, I know that things were not as I once chose to remember them. I can look through the rose-colored glasses I once wore and fantasize a beautiful childhood, or I can look through my dark glasses and perceive an exaggerated wretchedness of my childhood. Walking straight now, with clear vision, I know that my childhood was neither always negative nor always positive. At the time, though, I knew that things were not as they should have been. I didn't know what normal was; I only knew that things weren't right. So I guessed at what my thoughts and feelings should have been and disregarded what they really were. I denied my natural curiosity about life so as to hide the abnormalities from myself. The more I pushed my true feelings down inside of me, the less I liked my life.

Uncle Buddy

During the summers, I worked at the paper company where my mother worked, well into my teens. There were fun times for me, like when my Uncle Vern (whom I nicknamed Uncle

Buddy), tired as he was in the evenings, would take me over the Lake Overholster, and we would go fishing. I can remember the joy of sitting silently, waiting patiently for a tug on my line. My Uncle Vern inspired me to learn the art of listening and waiting for the right moment to catch the fish. He also taught me how not to lose the fish once I felt the tug on the line. I always took pride in the things I learned from my uncle; I developed personal qualities such as diligence, attentiveness and perseverance. I try to utilize these learned strengths daily, since they make life so much easier.

I now understand, looking back as an adult, that during my childhood and adolescence, the world was not the problem. The problem was how I related to myself. I had dreams and fantasies of what I was going to do with my life after high school, but my low self-opinion and low self-esteem degraded my motivation.

A Continuing Influence

As adolescents, my sister and I were sometimes up past midnight discussing life. And 99% of the time we ended up talking about our mother. I didn't realize at the time how much effect my mother had in my life. It wasn't until her death, much later, that I finally felt that I was free from it.

Marian "Pat" Benedict Cmdr. USN NC Ret.

The Silence of the Pain is Deafening

I used to look back on my childhood in anger and frustration. I now know that those kinds of feelings stem from feelings of inadequacy which are often found in alcoholics. It is common for alcoholics to feel insecure and inadequate. I was actually child-like on the inside while I seemed very mature on the outside. Sometimes this personality makeup in an alcoholic stems from blocking out things from one's childhood which were too painful to deal with. These things are delegated to the back burner, as it were, and one just goes on, as one must. I believe I was born with the ability to cope with life, but it was alcoholism which corrupted that. It was through sobriety that I got my abilities back, and I am stronger for it. The greatest gift I got in sobriety was the gift to me of myself.

Edna, circa 1977

My sister was a good person who had a love/hate relationship with our mother. It was Jane's relationship with our mother which destroyed her, emotionally and eventually physically. I am glad I was not around to see her dying of anorexia during the last few years of her life. I know my mother was cruel to her up until the end. My cousin Garnet visited Jane during the end of her life; she and Jane were close. Garnet told me that when she would find my sister sitting with tears streaming down her face, she knew that my mother had been there, to once again belittle and criticize. My mother would never put her arm around Jane, or give her a pat on the back, or say, "I love you." or "It's ok."

My sister, bless her soul, committed slow, painful suicide. She became anorexic and it lingered on for years. I noticed when she first started losing weight, but I was otherwise blind to Jane's condition. It probably registered with me that something was wrong with Jane, but either I was so wrapped up in my own problems, or I chose not to look at it. Simply put, I did not see it for what it was. I am particularly saddened because my sister was a better person than I. She was more forgiving, more understanding, more loving; she was smarter by far.

Jane

When we were teenagers, I wanted desperately for Jane to stand up to my mother, but she never really did. I never did

Marian "Pat" Benedict Cmdr. USN NC Ret.

either. My focus was on finishing school and getting out and on with my life. Jane just took our mother's abuse. Later in life, Jane would call our mother every morning just to see how she was, and my mother treated her like a dog.

A lesson in Honesty

When I was seven or so we lived just a few blocks from the school I went to and there was a Safeway grocery store in between. That grocery store became very special to me as a little girl, and although it has long since been gone, I still think fondly of it to this day.

But one time on the way home from school some classmates and I stopped by the store to swipe some candy bars. I got away with two Baby Ruth bars; they were five cents apiece back then. I ate the candy but I kept the wrappers in my jacket pocket.

I was playing in the living room when my mother got home from work. She picked up my jacket from where I had dropped it on the floor and threw it to me, saying, "Go hang this up."

The candy wrappers came out mid-air and fluttered to the floor. She picked them up and began to question me.

"Where did you get the candy?" she asked. I just froze, and she wouldn't let up. I said I got them at the store. "Where did you get the money?" she persisted.

I finally explained that the other girls stole candy so I did too, but that didn't get me off the hook. That excuse just made her angrier. Now I was really scared. I knew I was in big trouble.

My mother said, "Put on your jacket." She handed me the candy wrappers and we drove to the Safeway.

I walked in, candy wrappers in hand, crying, certain I was going to jail. My mother made me go to each employee and apologize, saying that I would pay for the candy bars with my allowance. Of course I did, and my allowance was gone for a while.

As my mother and I were walking out of the store, I looked back to see some of the employees laughing. That didn't make sense to me at the time, since it was such a traumatic event for me. But now I understand that my mother often went overboard in the area of punishment. It did work, however: that was the last time I stole.

Defending Mother

Once, when I was maybe twelve, my father came to our home in the evening. He and my mother had a big fight and he pushed her into the bathroom and began to hit her. I ran to the kitchen and got a big carving knife. I pushed the point of it into his back and shouted, "Let her go or I'll kill you!"

Marian "Pat" Benedict Cmdr. USN NC Ret.

He left immediately. Jane was shocked. She stood there like a wide-eyed zombie. But none of the three of us ever talked about that incident. It was many years later that Jane, just out of nowhere, asked if I would have stabbed him if he had continued to hit our mother.

My reply was plain, simple and honest: "Yes."

Mother's Sense of Humor

Recently I have thought about my mother. I have gone to her grave and just stood there, almost emotionless. The only thought that came into my mind was: "Well mother, I guess you did the best you knew how." In her own way, she did the best she could.

What I miss most about her is her humor; my mother could be very funny when she was in the mood. There was once when I was about 9 that I managed to talk my mother into going to the theatre with me. Part of what made that a challenge was that the feature film starred the Three Stooges, which didn't interest her. Once the film started, however, she began to laugh. I don't remember that I had ever heard her laugh so hard or for so long.

My mother kept her sense of humor to herself, in a sense, because she would say something so mater-of-fact and deadpan that you wouldn't know it was a joke at first. One time my sister was with her when she was going through some old clothes she had long since stopped wearing.

My sister asked about a garment: "How long will you keep *that*?

"When I die I'll send for it," was her reply.

One time my mother was telling my sister Jane, my cousin Bob and me of when she was young and she and my aunt Bobby and my aunt Eva all attended a one-room multi-grade school together. They would ride an old horse, Billy, to school each morning. Billy would then go back home, but when school let out, Billy would be there waiting, and the three of them would hop on for the trip home. I thought about that, and then later I asked her how Billy knew what time to return to the school in the afternoon. She said that Billy had a clock in the barn. It was a couple of days before I realized she was kidding me, and Bob and Jane were snickering a bit that it took me so long. But my mother's sense of humor was sometimes like that: subtle and dead-pan.

Sister Jane

My sister Jane married a man named Bob Chester when she was nineteen or twenty. She lost their first child, a boy, at seven months due to a pregnancy complication. A couple of years later she had Nancy by Cesarean section. I was a student nurse then at St. Anthony's hospital, and I helped with the

The Silence of the Pain is Deafening

Cesarean section in surgery. Nancy was a very healthy baby. A year or so later, when close to full term, Jane lost another baby boy. After about ten years of marriage, Jane's husband died of lung cancer.

The closest I remember my sister and I being, as far as communication, understanding, laughing and getter along, was when we were both drinkers. We each felt freer and more open after we had a few drinks; it was easier to share our feelings and emotions. Later, in January of 1975, when we were in our 40's and I had my mastectomy, my sister, despite being ill, got on a plane to L.A. and came to see me at the Long Beach Naval Hospital. She stayed two or three days and I was very touched at the time by her visit. She said she just wanted to see me to know that I was all right. My mother did not come. I really didn't care whether my mother came to see me or not; she chose not to.

After her husband died, my sister Jane worked at Christensen Diamond Products, a company that made the big drilling bits for oil companies. She was the only woman in the office. Among other things, she handled a large payroll. She was well-liked by her coworkers, as well as by everyone else.

Ordinarily Jane didn't take life so seriously; she would come and go with the punches. However, there was a decline in her desire to live at the time Bob died of cancer. I took a break from my training in Los Angeles, and we brought Bob home briefly during the Christmas holiday for his birthday. Bob turned 36 on Christmas day. He died on New Year's Day at St. Anthony's hospital.

My Adopted Nephew Len

Several years before Bob's death, he and Jane adopted Len, a part Cherokee Indian, when he was about five days old. Their daughter Nancy was then about five years old, and happy to get a baby brother. Although I was stationed elsewhere at the time, I happened to be home on leave when they found out, with three days' notice, that they could adopt him.

I remember going up to the University hospital to get Len. Since the birth mother and the adopted parents weren't allowed to meet, I am the only one in the family who has seen his mother. I remember her as a very pretty, dark-haired woman. In those days the mother would carry the child out of the hospital in her arms before giving it up. She made a comment to me that he looked a lot like his uncle, her brother. She handed him to me, and then she went one way and I went the other. Bob and Jane were waiting in the car and, by the time I got there, they had about gone crazy. They could hardly wait to get their hands on the boy.

I received Len and gave him to Bob and Jane on Saturday evening. Not until that Monday did they go to court to officially adopt him, allowing the birth mother time to reflect. Len's mother was to appear in court on Monday morning to sign the papers, and then Bob and Jane were to go there in the afternoon for their part. Over the weekend Bob and Jane were absolutely thrilled with this boy. My mother and my Aunt Bobbie came by to see him and they also were very pleased and happy for Bob and Jane. However, Jane's husband Bob suffered anxiety and fear that over the weekend Len's mother would change her mind. He worried that Jane would suffer loss and be disappointed. But while Bob worried so, Jane was very much together. She felt secure mentally, emotionally and spiritually. She said something to me along the lines of: "God wants us to have this boy, and he is ours." Jane had faith in the depths of her heart that the child was hers, so she was truly at peace.

Brother in Law Bob's Lung Cancer

About three years later, our family was devastated by the rapid decline in Bob's health, and then by his death from the lung cancer, at the age of 36. He was well-liked, and indeed loved by the entire family. He was an outgoing type of person, personable, happy and thrilled to death with his family. He had developed a cough. He looked healthy from outside appearances, and Jane had teased him and said, "If you don't go and get that cough looked at, I'm going to divorce you." He finally went in for an x-ray, returning to work afterwards. The doctor called their house, and Jane went over to look at the x-rays. The right lung was almost all gone, and part of the left lung had carcinoma. Jane called me in Corpus Christi; I drove all night, arriving the next day. I wanted to confer with the doctor, and discuss the matter with my family. Being the nurse, I felt like I had to stop my life and take care of others, especially my family. I later returned to Corpus Christi, received a hardship discharge from the Navy, thus resigned my commission, and then returned home.

So when Bob went in for a scaling node biopsy, (Dr. Alan Greer did it), the node was so enlarged they could not remove it from his neck. He was placed on chemotherapy (a nitrogen mustard compound which made people violently ill) until he died.

Bob's death was the beginning of my sister's decline. She filled her life with drinking and busying herself, which was probably just to avoid the grief. Jane married twice, and divorced shortly after each marriage. She never recovered from Bob's death; she was never the same. As I look back now on that period of our lives, I can see that she never allowed herself time to grieve. I think that many people, unfortunately, don't work through the grieving process and suffer as a result. From Jane's point of view, Bob was buried, everybody left,

Marian "Pat" Benedict Cmdr. USN NC Ret.

and so, life goes on. She had Nancy, who was about seven, and Len, who was about three, so she was able to stay busy.

I remember coming home from St. Anthony's hospital the day that Bob died. Len was on the couch, standing up at the window, and as I walked into the living room, he turned to me and said, "You let my father die in your hospital." That took me by surprise; it shocked me, really. His young mind was working through things, so I went over to the couch and took him into my arms. I don't remember what I said to him; it was unimportant since he was way too little to understand things.

Up until her husband's death, Jane had been living a dream, in a sense. She was living the ideal life of a housewife with two kids. All of a sudden that life was shattered. I don't believe that any of us are fully prepared for the death of a loved one. Bob died almost a year after being diagnosed, but even in the case of a long-term illness, when death is expected for several years, it can be very hard for someone to cope.

Jane seemed to cope with her husband's death fairly well after she got past those two quick marriages. She was probably trying to replace Bob in her life, which of course, didn't work. She would say that she wasn't angry at God for taking her husband so early in life. I think she bottled up her grief and tried to appear as if she were together. She eventually developed a drinking problem, which I just did not see at first.

My Story

Jane seemed to cope well, and she went on living, but inside, basically, she was dying. I believe that we all need to verbalize the joyous or sad, positive or negative events in our lives; we all need someone to talk to and share these events with. Even though Jane had two children she was still alone in the sense of not being able to share her innermost feelings with someone who might understand. Our mother was no help; she would just say, "Pick up your bed and walk," quoting what Jesus said to a paraplegic beggar. Of course, unlike Jesus and the beggar, my mother had not miraculously healed my sister, so this was no help. My sister simply could not do that. Jane needed adequate time to grieve and get past her husband's death and, based on my experiences in Vietnam, I know that she did not take sufficient time.

Cousin Bob's Understanding

I had very few intimate conversations with anyone except for my cousin Bob. Bob was the one person I spoke to, opened up to and deeply connected with during my childhood. We would go out to play, and even when we didn't talk much, we understood each other's feelings. Bob was able to understand what I was all about. I reciprocated with an understanding of Bob, and I accepted his worldly beliefs and strongholds.

Ordinarily I wouldn't try to make people understand me; a deep understanding wasn't usually the point of conversing.

Marian "Pat" Benedict Cmdr. USN NC Ret.

With cousin Bob, however, a deep understanding was there with or without the conversation.

We still understand

Childhood Delusions; Adult Reality

I wanted to be a part of the merry-go-round of life, but sometimes I also wanted to hop off in the center and let the world spin around me. I wanted to be the center of the world, while being separate from it, and Bob felt the same way. The two of us would fantasize that we were special and distinct from the world. This fantasy was almost a delusion of grandeur, and we felt uplifted by it. My cousin Bob, now wealthy and retired, had become a successful businessman. I am a retired Navy Commander, an associate university

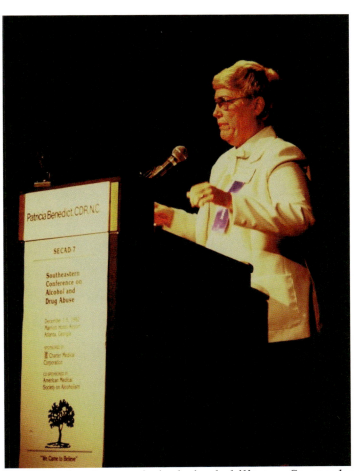

professor and a drug and alcohol rehabilitator. So maybe the mirage of greatness that was part of our childhood helped us to strive for greatness as young adults.

Marian "Pat" Benedict Cmdr. USN NC Ret.

Chapter Four
Nursing

The Silence of the Pain is Deafening

Patsy Lee

When I was about four and Jane was six, we lived with our mother in a duplex on the east side of Oklahoma City. We lived next door to a woman named Mrs. Benton. Our mother worked to support us, and so Mrs. Benton would babysit me while Jane was in school. It was Mrs. Benton who provided the precursor to my nick-name Pat. My mother said Mrs. Benton used to refer to me as Patsy Lee and sing my praises. She would talk about how Patsy Lee was so cute and so smart, and could do this and do that. She would say to my mother, "Edna, you have Jane to raise, and you've got this other child to raise, let me adopt Patsy, and I will raise her and make sure she gets a good education." My mother said that at first she felt horrified that somebody wanted to take her child away, and then she said that she was heart-warmed by the fact that Mrs. Benton was concerned with where my mother was going to get the money to raise us, and she truly cared about my welfare. My mother said Mrs. Benton offered many times to adopt me.

Early Scholar

My mother said that one day I tried to follow my sister to school and that she had to run and get me. We

Nursing

ll, Mother came home from work one day and asked Mrs. Benton how everything went, and Mrs. Benton said, "Oh, everything is just great. I enrolled Patsy in school today."

Mother said she sat back and thought to herself, "My God, the kid is four years old." She thought Mrs. Benton was just teasing her, because she had commented in the past about how smart I was.

And my mother said, "Oh my God, surely you didn't do that Mrs. Benton."

"Oh yes, I enrolled her in the first grade."

"She's not even five years old yet," My mother said.

"She will be soon and she tested higher than kindergarten level."

I didn't turn five until May, so I was always younger than all the kids in my class.

I was younger than my classmates, but I stayed with the best of them in grades. Later, in high school, I was ahead of my class in credits so that, the summer before my senior year, I realized I only needed three or four more credits to graduate. I decided I was just going to slide by during that summer; play instead of going to summer school. I thought I could just finish up my credits for my graduation during fall/winter session by going part time and then I would still graduate a half-year

Marian "Pat" Benedict Cmdr. USN NC Ret.

earlier than I was supposed to. Well, I thought that was a great plan, but things didn't work out that way.

No Rest for the Scholar

I had just turned 17, and I planned to get the rest that I thought I deserved. I contemplated a life of relaxation, concentrating only on the trivial things. I was going to coast through the summer and the fall. My mother approached me one day in May, shortly after my birthday. I'll never forget her words. She said, "You only lack three or four credits to complete high school. You are going to make a decision: you are either going to business school or college or you will do something about getting a job."

Nursing? Not for me, thanks.

Well, this came as a big shock. Shirley Booth, who lived three blocks down the road, had been my best friend since Seventh Grade. She also lacked three credits to graduate. We ran around together; her father would drop us off for roller skating on Saturday nights. Mr. Booth was like a surrogate father to me in those days. Shirley and I were like sisters; we belonged to the same pep club and we were inseparable. Coming home from Classen High School one afternoon that spring of 1947, we were discussing our futures. I thought I wanted to be a Physical Education teacher. I enjoyed sports; especially tennis. We were trying to decide who made the most

Nursing

money: teachers or nurses. I had never in my life dreamed of or contemplated becoming a nurse. I could not stand hospitals. I hated the smell of them and I didn't want to be near one.

When I was in my early teens I had very bad tonsillitis and Mother said she paid $20 to Dr. Townsend and his nurse to come out to the house because my tonsils were so bad. My mother did not have the money to put me in the hospital and I wouldn't have gone anyway. Ann, the nurse, dripped ether so that I would go to sleep and Dr. Townsend could take my tonsils out. I asked him to leave my tonsils on my dresser and when I woke up they were sitting on my dresser. I didn't think it was so odd at the time, but now, when I think of a physician performing surgery at home in my bed, I think: *"My God!"*

So, my initial response to Shirley's idea of a career in nursing was that it was the furthest thing from my mind. My sister Jane trained for nursing at a hospital in Oklahoma and I said to my sister Jane at the time, "Well, no one is going to get a pair of white stockings on me. You've got to be insane."

She lasted about six months. She said she was more interested in getting married, and having children so she dropped out of nursing school.

Well, God works in strange ways. I thought about nursing as I would about going out and planting a garden: "Who cares about that?" When Shirley and I discussed paychecks,

Marian "Pat" Benedict Cmdr. USN NC Ret.

however, we decided that nurses make more than teachers, and then we made the decision in about five minutes that we would become nurses.

So, I approached my mother and said that I would go to summer school and graduate from high school in August, and that Shirley and I had agreed to become nurses. Well, my God, I thought my mother was going to go into total shock. She looked at me and said, "Where did you ever come up with that idea?"

At the time, my mother wanted me to get an education on my own somehow, or to get out on my own and work, or to otherwise move out, because of the financial burden. My sister had moved out, I was still at home, and I too was looking forward to a little freedom. As a nursing student I would be able to be on my own, because in those days nursing students and nurses lived in special housing near the hospital.

So my dream of playing and doing nothing came to a screeching halt after my 17th birthday in May of 1947. Many of my classmates got part-time jobs that summer, while I went back to class to get my diploma. Despite her objection to Catholicism, my mother was agreeable to my entering St. Anthony's, a Catholic education system. I think that she hoped that the nuns would keep an eye on me while I studied and became a good nurse.

Nursing

In October of 1947, Shirley Booth and I enrolled at St. Anthony's to study nursing. However, I was neither enthused nor excited. I remember that at the time I had no idea why I was there. I eventually worked as a nurse for over forty years. It was a decision that I have never regretted; I fell in love with nursing.

I didn't have any apprehension about leaving home and enrolling in nursing school at the age of 17. But then, my mother had moved into an apartment across from St. Anthony's Hospital. So I wasn't quite on my own at first; I was still with my mother; all I had to do was walk across the street to enroll in nursing school. I also had the support of my best friend, Shirley Booth.

However, we were soon living in the student housing. All of us first year students lived three to a room (the second year students did as well). I lived with Shirley Booth and Delores, who later entered the Navy with me. There was some shuffling around in those first few weeks, and I ended up living with Anna Marie DeJacamo and Lou Alice Thompson. Shirley Booth and I remained good friends throughout our lives. Meanwhile, I became such good friends with Anna Marie and Lou Alice that by our senior year, even though we could live two to a room, we said we wanted to all three stay together. We did have to split up, though and I ended up rooming with

Marian "Pat" Benedict Cmdr. USN NC Ret.

a gal called 'Sporty' Davis, while Anna Marie and Lou Alice lived together.

During the first four months of the first year we did nothing but classroom work. We wore the white uniforms, the white stockings and the white shoes in school. It wasn't until January of 1948 that we were given our nursing caps, on Nurse's Cap Day. After we received our nurse's caps, we were allowed to go onto the floor in the hospital and begin nursing under supervision.

Living in the nurse's quarters was very exciting to me, as was working "on the floor" at the hospital. I felt as though I had entered adulthood. I thought that I was going to be another Florence Nightingale. I had found out Florence Nightingale was born on May 12th, 1820. So she and I have the same birthday, 110 years apart.

When I began to work as a nurse, however, I was still quite young and not ready emotionally and mentally to enter the field of nursing. I needed to gear myself not to become emotionally involved with patients. Nurses are trained caregivers, and sometimes we feel like trying to take care of the whole world all at once. Our feelings for our patients and our drive to make everything everywhere right can make nursing a very difficult profession. The mature nurse will keep such feelings and drives in check.

Nursing

Life, Death and Contentment

I remember one patient, Shirley Abernathy, a teenager. It was my junior year and Shirley Abernathy was dying of leukemia. Leukemia wasn't treated with chemotherapy or radiation like it is today; there was little research on cancer. Lou Alice, Anna Marie and I became emotionally attached to this young woman. In my mind's eye I can still see the private room she was in, and I remember now that her uncle was a fireman. Shirley Abernathy bled from her gums, from her nose and from her vagina. In those days all we did for leukemia victims was to provide them with blood transfusions. Shirley Abernathy was the first death that I recall experiencing as a nurse. When she died it was devastating to all of us. Shirley's death gave spiritual meaning to nursing for me. I began to contemplate life and death. If my first experience of death in nursing had been an elderly person, maybe it wouldn't have made the impact that Shirley's death did. Shirley's memory has remained in my heart all my life. As a result of her death, I began to mature emotionally and spiritually; I began to achieve the maturity I needed to be a nurse.

About five o'clock one evening, the Supervisor of Obstetrics, known to us as Costie, told me to scrub in and help Dr. Rogers deliver a baby. I had never scrubbed in and assisted in anything before. I will never forget seeing the birth of human life for my first time. I was thrilled to be helping Dr. Rogers, who was the Chief of Obstetrics. He ended up being a very dear and personal friend, not only to me but to my mother as well. Having seen that baby delivered and having heard the cry, I was more excited than ever about nursing. Having seen a birth and having experienced a death, my own life took on a new meaning. I knew then, in my heart, that nursing was for me. That was what I wanted to do the rest of my life, and with that knowledge, with that decision, came inner contentment.

Maxine: Entertainment on a Budget

We had study hall in the evenings from eight until nine. Mrs. Olden, the house mother, would sit at her desk, up on a little platform. She had the job of making sure we sat at our desks and stayed quiet, although she was elderly and not always aware of her surroundings. There was one time Mrs. Olden had no idea what was happening when Maxine snuck out the back door.

Most of the students were poor and just got by. I got five dollars a month, to use for clothing, books and miscellaneous needs. I recall that Anna Marie's dad, Peter DeJacamo, gave me underpants and stockings one year, and that was a big help. We didn't have to pay for food or housing, but still, there was little money left for entertainment, so we used to tease Maxine, just to liven things up. Maxine would always have runs in her stockings and she absorbed a lot of teasing for the way her clothes looked.

One time Maxine came to class late. She had on her white uniform, her white stockings with massive runs in them, and high heels, which were against regulations. She had hooked a string on an empty Kotex box and wore it on her arm like a purse. She came into the classroom just when we got ready to settle down and study. Maxine quietly tip-toed in those high-heeled shoes, so Mrs. Olden wouldn't notice anything. With the runs in her stockings and the Kotex box for a purse, Maxine was a complete disruption. We tried so hard not to laugh that the tears ran down our cheeks. She quietly breezed in, looking serious, like nothing was up. Maxine set her Kotex box down like it was her purse and took out her pencil and started to study. Mrs. Olden never saw what happened, but we all about fell on the floor.

The Fiddle

Across the street from the nursing school at St. Anthony's was a bar. I don't remember the exact name of the bar; only that we called it 'The Fiddle'. At the time Oklahoma was a dry state, so all they served at the bar was beer. Starting when I was still 17, we would go over and get a bottle of beer and play shuffle board and listen to the juke box. Beer was only a dime and we went there for some relaxation; that was our only outlet for recreation. There was a Chiropractic school down the street and a lot of the chiropractic students used that bar. Some of the student nurses dated some of the student Chiropractors. Sometimes we would sneak out to The Fiddle and have a beer before going to bed. The good sisters had only to look out the window to see us, and would know where we were going. I'm sure they just allowed it.

During the first year, I began to settle into a life of nursing. I enjoyed the freedom of living in the nurse's residence, but some of my classmates and I would go across the street to where my mother lived. My mother was still talking about those days right up until her death. She talked of coming home from work at 5:30 and never knowing what she would find. One student nurse would be in the back room washing her hair, and another would be in the kitchen cooking food. Another nurse would be sewing and someone else would be studying. My mother remembered nearly having to step over bodies when she came home. She loved it. All her life, my mother loved and respected nurses, and for that I am very proud.

Being a nursing student wasn't easy; we rotated working one of three shifts: 7 am to 3 pm; 3 to 11 pm and 11 pm to 7 am. We worked whatever shift and whichever days we were told. No one consistently got weekends off, and during our junior year, we did not get any days off. However sometimes a student nurse would finish her shift at 3 PM one day and not start her next shift until 3 PM the next day. We called that an overnight. It was a 24 hour break, which was a big deal to us. When we worked overnight, we still had to attend classes. Sometimes, when there was a shift change, a student nurse would have no time for rest in between shifts; other times the shift change would allow for some time off. At times we wanted to quit and forget about nursing, but my mother would encourage us to stay the course. My mother backed us, encouraged us, and gave us the strokes we needed to get through those difficult three years of our lives.

While in school, I began taking instructions in Catholicism, which my mother was very much against. I became a Catholic, was baptized and have remained one to this day. That was another life decision which I have never regretted. My mother and I worked out our religious differences over the years. Perhaps at first she was worried that I would become a nun, but eventually she accepted that I was Catholic. My first Catholic missal ever was given to me by my Aunt Faye on one of my birthdays.

Heavy Drinking and a Stillborn Nephew

One time Anna Marie and Lou Alice and I attended a party on one of our overnights. The party was at one of the Chiropractic student's home. The students wanted to drink hard liquor. Oklahoma was dry at the time and so we called the bootlegger and he brought over a bottle of whisky. We also had some beer. It was my first experience with heavy drinking. When we would go over to The Fiddle, we did not get drunk. We would go have a beer, laugh, play shuffle board and go back to the nursing quarters. But that evening, we ordered a bottle of bootleg whisky. Then we sat in a circle and drank boiler makers; that is: we would pass the bottle around, and each take a drink of whisky, followed by a swallow of beer. I became very drunk. At one point I got up to go to the bathroom and I fell against the stove and broke the gas pipe. Gas was leaking out. I thought that was very funny. We got a potato and cut it in half and jammed the end of it to stop the gas from leaking out. Sometime later that night I got very sick. I was 18 years old and I had had no experience with heavy drinking. I remember vomiting and vomiting and vomiting. In fact, later in life I became known as a pukee because I puked so much when I got too drunk.

When we got back to the nurses quarters after the party I was shaking and sweaty and very nauseated even though I had nothing more to throw up. I was trying to keep some juice down to get myself together to go to work in obstetrics. I worked in the nursery from 3:00 to 11:00, and from three o'clock on, I prayed for the time to go by quickly. The room was still spinning, and I just wanted to get off duty and crawl into my bed and lay my head down.

The whole afternoon and evening I said over and over, "I will never, ever do that again."

At around 10 that night, I was thinking to myself that I had only one more hour to work, and then I could go sleep off my hangover. Then Rose, the night supervisor, got a phone call from my brother-in-law that they were bringing in my sister. She was almost at full term in her pregnancy. She was hemorrhaging. That jarred me awake and sobered me up. She had a total placental abruption; that is: the placenta became detached from the uterine wall. They typed and cross-matched her for blood and started a transfusion. There were still some faint, irregular heartbeats from the fetus. We took my sister Jane into surgery to do an emergency caesarian section. The obstetrician delivered a stillborn baby boy.

My mother, my aunt and my brother-in-law were there. My sister was in shock. By the time she was stabilized and out of surgery and back into her room (we did not have recovery rooms in those days), it was around two or three o'clock in the morning. I was very tired, very frightened and very hung-over. One of the sisters took me down to the kitchen to get something to eat. A couple of the nurses said I looked bad, and they attributed my condition to the scare and trauma I had just experienced and I allowed that lie.

In reality, I was hung over and I was in the withdrawals of alcohol. My physical shape had nothing to do with what my sister had gone through, but I allowed that lie, even though I knew that the lie, the excuse for my hung over condition, was a precursor of self-destruction. Lying to cover drunkenness or a hangover leads to more drinking, and more lies. I went to the kitchen, I ate, and I went over to the nurses' quarters and went to bed. A few days later, we buried the baby. That one experience was a cure for me. I thought that women who get drunk are no different than sluts or whores, and so I did not want to be a female drunk. From that night, for many years, I abstained from drinking.

Psychiatric Training at the University of Oklahoma

As my nursing education progressed, I spent part of my senior year taking psychiatric education at the University of Oklahoma. We were there for three months in the spring of 1950. At that time, three months of psychiatric training was required on national boards as part of our nursing education. There was no such training available at St. Anthony's hospital.

One group of nurses went to a psychiatric hospital at Halstead, Kansas. I was in another group with Anna Marie and Lou Alice. We moved to Norman, Oklahoma and stayed on

Nursing

what was called the north naval base. During WWII, there was a naval base in Oklahoma, despite the fact that it is an inland state. We lived in the old naval barracks and we rode a bus over to the mental institution at Norman every day. I did not like psychiatry at all, although I made my best grade on the psychiatry part of the board exam.

I was later reminiscing with my good friend Anna Marie, and she reminded me that, when we smoked at the base (all of us smoked in those days) we would walk around with an ash tray in our hand to avoid a fire. The building was probably condemned. It was just an old wooden WWII barrack and would likely have burned to the ground in a matter of minutes.

There was one good thing about being at the University of Oklahoma in Norman. It was that my cousin, Bob Keller, attended the U of OK there at that time. At one point he dated my roommate, Lou Alice Compton. Even though I didn't see him a lot, having Bob nearby was strengthening for me. I was further from home then, still young, and I needed to have a close friend nearby. Bob eventually got married while he was still attending the University (I had to buy the engagement ring, since he was broke, and of course he never paid me back).

Bob Keller had a good friend, Bill Ziegler. We called him Little Billy, and sometimes, when the three of us had a weekend off, we would ride to Oklahoma City in Billy's old jalopy. The three of us would have a blast in the City. That was before Bob got married. Bill Ziegler eventually married a nurse that I knew and became an architect and now lives in Florida.

First Surgery and First Delivery

I remember the first time I was in surgery with Phyllis Bloomer, we scrubbed in on a case. It was for Dr. Lincolnfelter. I didn't know how to set up the table for surgical tools; in fact, I barely knew how to scrub in or how to assist. I liked surgery, but my love was Obstetrics.

My cousin Gordon, whom I was extremely fond of, had gotten married while he was in military service and his wife came to St. Anthony's on the 1st of August, 1950 to have their first child. I scrubbed in for the delivery, under the supervision of Dr. McKee. He made the preliminary vaginal incision (episiotomy) and then sat me down so I could deliver my first baby, Gordon's son Wayne. So I delivered my first baby on August 1st, shortly before I graduated in October of 1950.

A Tragedy and a Lawsuit

During my first year as a nursing student, when I was on night duty, an incident occurred which caused me to rethink my career choice. I had a patient who had a thyroidectomy done. Her daughter had worked for my father some years before that, but I had never met either the patient or her

Nursing

daughter. The patient became disoriented after her operation. She got out of bed and I had to put her back. Some private duty nurses walked by her room and so I asked if they would periodically check to make sure she was in bed. I called one of the physicians, an intern, and asked him to come see her. He ordered medication for her. There were side rails on the bed. Her room was on the second floor. I was trying to keep an eye on her the best I could.

When I was getting medications for other patients, one of the private nurses came up and said, "Mrs. McCoy is not in her room."

I said, "What do you mean she's not in her room?"

She said, "Pat, she's not in her room."

And I said, "She couldn't have gotten past me, except maybe when I was here in the medicine closet."

We checked her room and found the side rails on her bed still up. We searched for Mrs. McCoy without success. As I was about to call Sister Veronica, the night supervisor, the phone rang. It was Sister Veronica, who told me that Mrs. McCoy was in the emergency room. She had jumped out of the second story window. When she hit the ground a private duty nurse heard the impact, looked out the window and then called Sister Veronica. I was devastated and frightened. I wanted to quit. I thought to myself, "I'm not gonna look at

Marian "Pat" Benedict Cmdr. USN NC Ret.

this; I don't want nursing; let me out; this is not for me; I can't stand this." I went over to my mother's place. She had a tough job talking me into staying in nursing school.

Mrs. McCoy was paralyzed by the fall. She had two years to file a lawsuit and a couple of days before the two years were up, she filed. I was scrubbed in for Surgery when Sister Cecelia came and pulled me away. She brought me out and a sheriff handed me a subpoena to give a deposition and to appear in court. I was still a student at that time.

I went to court and was sworn in. One thing I remember was being asked why, if a sleeping pill had been ordered by Dr. Forster, wasn't Mrs. McCoy asleep.

I answered, "Some people sleep and some don't."

I was under the spotlight, but the hospital was the target. The fact that a young student nurse had responsibility for a number of patients was used to show negligence. The hospital settled by waiving all charges for the two years Mrs. McCoy spent there and by paying out some money. Mrs. McCoy wasn't discharged until the lawsuit was finally resolved.

The episode with Mrs. McCoy had such an impact that I nearly dropped out of school. That would have been the end of my career as a nurse. I stayed in school however, and testifying in court turned out to be a good learning experience for me,

Nursing

since I was later involved in a lawsuit while I served in the military.

Bootlegging Nurses

Sometime, toward the end of my schooling, I became good friends with a laboratory student, Juanita Michael. Juanita had a physician friend who ran a so-called alcohol hospital in Oklahoma City, where patients were weaned slowly from their addiction to alcohol. He needed a supply of liquor for that process and Oklahoma was still a dry state. He was buying from bootleggers, so Juanita and I saw an opportunity to make some money.

Juanita and I would drive down to Wichita Falls, a city on the other side of the Texas border. There we would go to a liquor store and buy one or two cases of liquor (that's all they would sell at one time). On occasion, a liquor store would sell us more than the maximum allowed. Different lots went to different liquor stores, so on those occasions we would cut the lot numbers off of the case boxes so that they couldn't be traced. On each trip we went from store to store until we had ten or fifteen cases and then we drove back. Juanita and I were not drinkers, so we sold all we brought back.

We made some ten trips to Texas in the course of time and sold the liquor mostly to doctors. I saved my share of the money we made and used it to buy my first car after I graduated. I first told my estranged father that I was now a registered nurse and I needed a car. He told me to save up and buy one. Neither of my parents were much help to me after I graduated. Two of my uncles had a Chevrolet dealership in Yukon. My uncle Ted was the one who sold me the dealer demo car, a two-toned green Chevrolet. I found out later that he practically gave me the car, selling it to me for such a low price.

Restlessness

When I graduated in October of 1950, I had no direction in my life. I didn't know what I wanted to do, now that I was a nurse. I worked in Obstetrics for a couple of years, which I loved. But as much as I loved it, I became restless. I could see no future for my career at St. Anthony's hospital. I was the float supervisor in obstetrics, which meant I worked whenever the regular supervisor was off, but I felt at the time that I would not advance any further anytime soon.

So it was in 1952 that Delores Femer and I began to talk about going into military service. I had a brother-in-law who had served in the Navy. He was then recalled for a year during the Korean War, and he later served a tour of duty in Kodiak, Alaska. He and I talked about my future, and he strongly influenced my decision to join the Navy. Delores Femer and I talked about going to Fort Hood, Texas to join the Army; I

Nursing

don't remember whether we discussed the Air Force. But we eventually agreed to join the Navy. Meanwhile, in July of 1952, I helped deliver my cousin Garnet's second child, Lois Anne. I like to tease Lois Anne today that she is so perfect because I delivered her. In all, I helped bring two of my cousins' children into the world. It was a very moving experience for me each time I helped bring a relative into the world, but for all of that, I was still restless.

Join the Navy and See the World

It was after the summer of 1952, after Lois Anne was born, that Delores and I flew to Dallas and joined the Navy Nurse Corp. My mother voiced no opposition to my decision. My life as a nurse at St. Anthony's was going well, so she didn't think that I was running away from problems or joining the service for some other bad reason. In retrospect, I was bored and I wanted to see the world and face new challenges; in other words, I was restless. It wasn't patriotism that prompted me to serve; it was more that I was twenty-two and full of youthful wants and needs. I could join the Navy and see the world: that was my outlook. So Delores and I were sworn into the Navy in October of 1952.

Marian "Pat" Benedict Cmdr. USN NC Ret.

The Silence of the Pain is Deafening

Training in St. Albans, NY

We boarded the plane to go to New York City as Navy Nurses. I had never been that far in my life. I put on the big front of knowing what I was doing, but we were so dumb about things. We were to report to the naval hospital in St. Albans, a neighborhood in Queens County, Long Island, not far from the NY airport. Delores and I had a one month orientation there.

We were taught Navy language and Navy ways. We were so green, and so uneducated on these things. We also received our uniforms at St. Albans. I felt very proud in my uniform; I had one stripe; I was an ensign, and I was on top of the world. My sister was married and doing well; she had a life. While I was at St. Anthony's hospital, I felt like I didn't really have a life. I entered the Navy with high hopes for my life, and I have never regretted that.

My Story

Nursing

We had a marine sergeant who had a purple heart from being wounded in Korea. He had the task of teaching some thirty of us in an indoctrination class. He tried to be very military about it all, but we were a bunch of young, giggly, twenty-something women. The man probably prayed to go back to Korea. It seemed as though he eventually let his guard down and said to himself, "Oh to hell with it. They'll never learn it anyway." But we were good friends with him.

Bainbridge, Maryland

After our month of Navy training in St. Albans, Delores Femer and I took a train to Bainbridge, Maryland which was my first duty station. It was a recruiting base at the time; they also had a fire-fighting school there. We lived in the nurse's barracks, which were very much like the old WWII Navy barracks I had lived in for my psychiatric training in Norman, OK.

I worked on a medical floor at the base. A young lieutenant nurse whom I worked for married an army officer, a graduate of West Point. Their wedding was at West Point, where I was her maid of honor. It was a great thrill for me to see the United States Army Academy at West Point. It was something to behold. I remember that the bride's last name was Pont, but I don't remember her first name and I don't know where she wound up.

Marian "Pat" Benedict Cmdr. USN NC Ret.

Restlessness Continues

Delores and I were stationed at Bainbridge, MD for two years. Delores had a red convertible, which we drove to Oklahoma when we were on leave during those two years. At the end of those two years, I left the Navy. I loved the Navy; I had no complaints about the Navy. I dated corpsmen even though we were not supposed to date enlisted men. I got along with everybody. But I was restless inside and dissatisfied with my life, as I had been throughout my youth. I was not homesick; there was nothing to come back to. I just wanted to go back to Oklahoma City. So I was honorably discharged in 1954, and I returned to Oklahoma City, to a boring and stale life. I worked, of course, and I was able to pay my mother back for all she had spent while I studied to be a nurse. I also bought her the first new car she ever owned, and a TV among other things. She never thanked me for any of it. Later, when she retired, I paid her bills so she could live more comfortably on Social Security.

The Seeds of Alcoholism

I was a drinker in those days, but not a heavy drinker. Still, I think that drinking played a role in my restlessness and discontentment with day to day life. I would occasionally drink at the officer's club at the base in Bainbridge, MD; I would have just a few drinks, like everyone else. I was

Nursing

dissatisfied with my life, but also with myself. It was as if I was seeking something, but I didn't know what.

I think that alcohol use fed my restlessness, and it was my restlessness which caused me to drink. I eventually drank to the point of self-destruction, as my drinking spiraled out of control. I could change the world, so it seemed, with a drink. Of course, the world did not really change; only my perceptions changed. So then, as early as my twenties, the seeds of alcoholism were sprouting.

Marian "Pat" Benedict Cmdr. USN NC Ret.

Chapter Five
Africa:
A Call to Serve and to Learn

The Silence of the Pain is Deafening

*M*y decision to go to Africa as a member of the Lay Missionary Helpers of Los Angeles was not a simple one. One thing I was thinking was that it is better to risk doing something, and have it not work out, than to get old and regret that I didn't do something, or at least try something I wanted to do, while I was still young and able. I was restless. I wanted to go somewhere far away, like Africa, just to see how things were over there. But most of all I wanted to do something good for other people. That desire, the desire to do good for others was a spiritual drive as much as it was just part of who I was (and still am). I believe that God called me to go; that is: I went there for Him; not in the sense that I went out of fear of Him, but that it was God who gave to me and inspired within me the desire to help others.

I don't recall whether I read about, or whether I had heard about the Missionary Helpers Association, which was founded by Monsignor Anthony Browers. At that time they were not looking for Priests, Nuns, Ministers or other Roman Catholic Church leaders, but instead they wanted lay people, practicing Catholics, who had other skills to offer. In my case, of course, that was nursing.

Much like what John F. Kennedy later proposed, The Peace Corp, The Lay Missionary Helpers of Los Angeles were recruiting people in various fields to come to Los Angeles for

Africa: A Call to Serve and to Learn

psychological testing and, for those who passed that, a year of training. The chosen recruits would then serve overseas somewhere, mostly in Africa, for three years.

Years don't make an individual smarter or wiser. Years only make one older. I was blessed in 1958 to be given the opportunity to look inside myself and to ponder what I wanted to do with my life. As I contemplated the death notices in the paper, I wondered why so many people didn't have the guts to just get out and do something with their lives. I was eager and ambitious. I felt a great desire to go and do something for mankind. Knowing that I would go do something for others brought me inner peace. It wasn't so much that I was doing something for the Catholic Church, it was that I wanted, as a nurse, to do something for other people.

I remember talking to my mother about this at the time. She was asking why I wanted to go do this, to go to Africa for three years after going to Los Angeles for a year of studying the customs and the language of the country where I would be going. I also had to get a job in L.A. to support myself while I trained. I don't know why I recall my response to my mother so vividly. It's not funny, but in a way it is. Mother asked me why I wanted to do that and in a mundane way I replied, "Well, Mother, I must be about my Father's business."

Editor's note: For those not familiar, when Jesus was about twelve Joseph and Mary were returning home from Jerusalem

Marian "Pat" Benedict Cmdr. USN NC Ret.

when they realized Jesus was not with them. They went back in a panic, searching for him, and after three days they finally found him in the temple, learning from the teachers. Astonished, they rebuked Jesus, who replied that they should have known that it was time for him to be about his Father's business. Coming of age, a young man would be about his natural father's business (e.g. carpentry). Mary and Joseph didn't quite understand what Jesus meant (See Luke chapter 2 verses 41 and following). So yes, Pat's statement to her mother was humorous (and, I believe, accurate).

But deeply and truly, that's what I felt. It's the same feeling I had, the same reason why I later worked with hard-core street people and gangs. We are all a part of humanity, God's children. God's people are found everywhere. That was the feeling that I had: that I wanted to go do something.

My brother in law Bob had terminal lung cancer. I had resigned my commission from the Navy to care for him, so I was free to pursue civilian interests. I had been taking care of Bob while he endured nitrogen mustard treatments, a rudimentary precursor to modern chemotherapy. Bob was inoperable and terminal. I knew that I could be of no more help to him by staying in Oklahoma City, in essence, waiting for him to die. I discussed this at length with my mother and with my sister. I made up my mind to join the Lay Missionary Helpers. I prayed over this a lot. Finally, I took pen in hand and I wrote to Los Angeles, to the Lay Missionary Helpers Association, to Monsignor Browers. I asked how to join.

Africa: A Call to Serve and to Learn

I got an application back. There was a questionnaire, and I was required to take the MMPI psychological test (the Minnesota Multiphasic Personality Inventory test). I paid for the test, which I took at the University of Oklahoma in Norman. I didn't see the test results; those went to Msgr. Browers. But I was accepted. I quit my job in Oklahoma City, and I drove my little Volkswagen to Los Angeles to check in at the Chancery's office to begin studying to go to Africa.

Soon after I arrived, I was entering Monsignor Browers' office when I met a woman named Marge Colino. We just happened to enter his office at the same time. She was a secretary from Cleveland, Ohio. She too was joining the Lay Missionary Helpers. We looked at each other and she asked, "You wanna be roommates?" I was starting to ask the same thing at the same time she did, and so we both together said, "Yes!" We became friends almost instantly. We found an apartment which suited us both.

I went to a nurse's registry in the area, a kind of employment office for nurses. There were plenty of nursing jobs, but I wanted more of a medical office-type job so I would be off evenings and weekends for study. I wound up with one of the best jobs I've ever had. I worked for Dr. Howard P. House, an ear surgeon. His office was across from St. Vincent's Hospital in Los Angeles. He was a great guy. The people I worked with there were great. I told them up front that I would only be there for a year, that I would be studying weekends and evenings with the Lay Missionary Helpers there in Los Angeles and that I was hoping to go overseas. They were good with all of that.

I studied in Los Angeles under Msgr. Browers, in conjunction with the Archdiocese of Los Angeles, which was under Cardinal James Frances Macintyre. Monsignor Browers ran the Lay Missionary Helpers Association under Cardinal Macintyre. During the week I took evening courses in theology and philosophy, as well as courses on the customs of the Masai, an African tribe. I began learning the language of Kiswahili (That is: Swahili; Ki is a Bantu prefix: *language of* -Ed). I attended classes three evenings during the week, and on Sunday. On Saturday nights I worked at St. Anne's Home for unmarried girls. I was a volunteer, working in the delivery room under supervision, so I could learn more about obstetrics and gain needed experience, which sometimes went beyond things a nurse would do in this country. This training led to my becoming a certified midwife in Africa.

I started to work for Dr. House in the fall of 1959. A few days before Christmas, I got a call from my sister Jane. She told me her husband Bob was critical. Dr. House gave me some time off to travel. At the time my father was working up

Africa: A Call to Serve and to Learn

north in California, so I called him and he drove down to Los Angeles to pick me up. We drove straight through to Oklahoma City. Bob had come home for Christmas, which was also his birthday. On the day after Christmas, Bob was returned to the hospital. He later lost consciousness, and I went to Mass and prayed for God to take him. My father, who had taken me to Mass then picked me up and took me back to the hospital. On New Year's Day, Bob died. I stayed at the hospital to help make some arrangements for his funeral. After Bob's funeral service, I returned to Los Angeles. Dr. House paid me my full salary. The man never took a day of pay from me, for which I was very grateful.

After I studied in Los Angeles for a year, I returned to Oklahoma City. My Uncle Ted put my little Volkswagen in the garage at his Chevrolet dealership in Yukon. He prepared it for extended storage so that I would have a car to drive when I returned from the mission. I flew to New York, and then to Copenhagen, Denmark. On the plane, on the way to Copenhagen from New York, it suddenly hit me. I thought, "My God, what am I doing going to Africa?" It had finally sunk in.

I traveled with my roommate Marge Colino. On our way to Africa, we went to Rome, where we had an audience with Pope John Paul XXIII. We, amongst the crowd, saw him in the

Sistine Chapel in Rome. We then went to Cairo and rode camels to the Sphinx. From there we flew to the Sudan, then I flew to Tobora, which was in Tanganyika. Tanganyika was under British administration until 1961; its name was changed

Marge and I

to Tanzania in 1964. My destination, at that time, was to be the Impanda Mission, which was approximately 80 miles from the Congo.

The town of Impanda was about one block square. The hospital, which was about five miles away, consisted of two old European houses, which had been converted for medical use. There were about 40 beds total, with no sheets. Some beds had old blankets; others just had a mattress. By tradition, the men were in one house and the women were in the other. The women would usually be accompanied by their extended families and their children. A third house was occupied by

Africa: A Call to Serve and to Learn

Sister Dr. Pauline Hilliard, who was from Ireland. She was a member of the Medical Missionaries of Mary from Drogheda, Ireland and was also a board qualified surgeon. The other lay missionary there was Fran Laterza. She was a physiotherapist from Los Angeles. Five miles back in town, at the Impanda Mission, lived three Fathers who were from Holland. Their religious order was called the White Fathers. Also, there were a couple of priests and a brother and then Fran, Sister Pauline, myself, and another lay missionary sister. For about 250 miles radius, that's all the white people there were. Father William and Father Brouchard and Father John were the names of the priests there.

Fran

At the house where we stayed we had two African house boys who knew very little English: Fostino, the African boy who cleaned the house, and Apolonari, a cook who cooked on

Marian "Pat" Benedict Cmdr. USN NC Ret.

a wood stove. We needed fluency in Kiswahili in order to communicate with them. Someone who knows Kiswahili could also speak, or at least understand, Kiha and Kefeepa, which were dialects or derivatives of Kiswahili.

Our hospital staff was not segregated. We had a Muslim, a Pagan and we had three Christians. Maria was an African girl who ran our pharmacy. She had what would be a fourth grade education in America. Veronica, who was another African  woman, worked in the hospital with us and had the equivalent of a sixth grade education. They were terrific people, and each with an endearing sense of humor. Teresa also worked with us. She was an African registered nurse, having received a two year course in nursing from the White Sisters in Kenya.

I'm glad I studied Swahili. I would have been isolated otherwise. It was easier for me to understand what others were saying than it was for me to reply in their language, but I was able to communicate. In the Kabanga Mission, some 230 miles to the north, the Kefeepa dialect was spoken; thirty miles to the south of us the Kiha dialect was preferred. Thankfully, I was fluent enough in Kiswahili to handle those dialects as well.

I went to work immediately upon my arrival. I was the first and the only assistant to Sister Dr. Pauline. We did surgery in the morning and ran a clinic in the afternoon. Our surgeries started at 7:00 in the morning, due to the heat (often over 110 degrees in the afternoon). We waited until 7 am to start because we operated by sunlight. We waited for it to come through the window. As the sun moved during the morning, we would move the operating table next to a different window, to maintain more direct sunlight on it. We did caesarean sections, we did thyroidectomies, hysterectomies, gastrectomies and appendectomies, among others. My job was to deliver all the babies and to learn to extract teeth. So, I became, in essence, a dentist as well as a midwife.

In our clinic we saw some 50 or 60 patients a day. There were a lot of cases of malaria; we also treated dysentery, hook worm and sleeping sickness, among other ailments. Most of the patients who arrived at our clinic expected something, even if they were not ill, so we tried to appease them with a check-up and maybe some vitamins or other harmless pills.

Most of our medications were drug samples which were forwarded to us from European (mostly German) doctors. So, many of my evenings were spent with a pile of drug samples and a German-English dictionary, trying to determine what the medications were. I would then try to write the equivalent English next to the German, as best I could, to avoid mix-ups. Some drug samples came from Oklahoma City. I don't remember their names, but there were some doctors in Oklahoma City who supported me and sent some of their samples.

One pleasant surprise upon my arrival was being addressed as 'mama' by most everyone. They would say, "Jambo, mama, habari gani?" Which means, "Hello, mama, how are you?" Once I adjusted to being called mama (having never had children, the moniker was new to me) I really liked it.

At first I was using an old wooden fetal scope. I would place one end to my ear and the other to the pregnant woman's abdomen to listen to the fetal heartbeat. It was really quite primitive. I wrote to my doctor friends in Oklahoma City, and an ordinary fetal scope was sent to me. I learned to work without electricity or running water. I delivered babies on a kitchen table in the old European house-come-hospital. There was one time an African woman was about ready to deliver her baby when she jumped up off of the kitchen table and ran off into the bush. I was astonished and scared. I went back over to the hospital that night, wondering if she would return. I

Africa: A Call to Serve and to Learn

woke Sister Dr. Pauline, but she wasn't perturbed that this African mother-to-be had darted off into the bush. The next morning the woman came back with the baby in her arms. She was extremely upset, panicked and frightened. The baby had bilateral clubbed feet (a correctable birth defect) and this African woman thought that she had caused this by running off to deliver. It took Sister Pauline quite a while to calm this woman down and to explain things to her. We put little plaster casts on the baby's feet and reassured her that in no way was she a sinner. She fully believed that she had done wrong before God and appeared on the verge of just giving this child to us. During my time there we received no requests for abortions, and we preformed none; childbearing was simply part of life for the Africans.

Most Africans didn't want charity, so to help their pride, we would charge them a small fee. We charged a couple of shillings for them to come to the clinic or be in the hospital. Seven shillings equaled one dollar at that time. If we delivered a baby and the woman had no shillings, she or her husband would bring three or four eggs or some fruit. They would pay with something, and thus we allowed them to keep their pride. I really cannot recall ever that an African did not thank us. Whatever we did for them in the hospital or in the clinic, or down at the mission at the church, they repeatedly said, "santi sana" thank you, thank you.

At Mass, the collections were interesting. Once a man put in a shilling and took some change out of the collection box. I was taken aback the first time I saw this, then I thought, "Well, that's alright. I've actually thought about doing that myself." In fact, I've seen it done in United States. He only had so much money, he put money in and took out his change. Also, they'd put apples, oranges, eggs or whatever else in the collection box at church.

Many of our patients had little or no experience with medications. When Maria worked in the pharmacy, she might tell a patient to take one pill in the morning, or maybe one at noon, and one at night. She came to us one day, extremely perturbed. She was shaking her head and waving her arms. Sister Pauline had to calm her down so she could tell us what the problem was. She'd given a woman thirty-six tablets and told her to take them in the morning, at noon, and at night. The woman took all thirty-six tablets right then, expecting to receive more later. Thank God they were vitamin tablets.

Africa: A Call to Serve and to Learn

One day Sister Pauline and I went down to the Chala Mission on some business. There was an African Bishop who lived in Chala, Bishop Imsekila. He was educated and spoke English. He was also quite ill. Sister Pauline told him that she thought that he might have appendicitis. We drew some blood and found that his white blood count was elevated. That would be the case if he had appendicitis. Educated or not, he still had his primitive upbringing and was mistrustful of modern medicine. He was a nice guy and remained very pleasant while he and Sister Pauline discussed at length that he probably needed to have his appendix out. But he decided to go home, thinking he would get over it. Sister Pauline could not talk him into the needed surgery.

Around two o'clock in the morning, the bishop, painfully ill, returned to the hospital. We took two land rover trucks and drove them up the windows, so that the headlights could provide the necessary light, and Pauline took out a very bad appendix, one that was about to rupture (which might have proved fatal).

I arrived in Africa at a time of year when the daytime temperatures were typically over 110 degrees. I liked the answer I gave my mother when she asked why I would do such a thing as go to Africa on missionary work, and so, when others would ask, I repeated this same answer: "I must be about my Father's business." I began to say that with pride and self-confidence, which are great enemies of Christianity (human pride and self-confidence belittle God and exalt ourselves above Him, though God is the Sine-Qua-Non of us -Ed). With the heat, poverty and primitive conditions, I was properly humbled before God within a matter of days of my arrival. When I realized what my working conditions would be like, my quest to be an African missionary lost its glamour.

When I took the time from my work as a nurse to look deep into the eyes of the Africans, I realized that they, like all of humanity, need not only to be loved, but to be told and shown that they are loved. I think that when we do nothing in this world, the silence, the lack of love, grows beyond the bounds of life and death. I have never regretted going on the mission. I have regretted many things in my life, but I have never regretted that experience. In Africa, I quickly came to realize what humanity is really all about. It is not the material things, or even the creature comforts. When you look into the eyes of

Africa: A Call to Serve and to Learn

any human being, whether they are in Africa or sitting at a nightclub in New York, when you see in their eyes vacancy or a vacant look, then internally the person is dying. That is what I saw in the eyes of some Africans: a person dying. Not so much from a lack of food, but from not knowing that they were loved. All of mankind needs love. The silence of doing nothing is deafening. That is what I came to realize in Africa.

A day or two after Sister Pauline removed the appendix of the bishop, the Volkswagen, the one we drove down there in, was loaded full for the trip back to the Impanda Mission. I said I wanted to return to the Impanda Mission by bus. I wanted the experience. And an experience I got.

Let me just say: a greyhound bus, it wasn't. I was the only white person on the bus, which left Chala at about twelve noon and did not get to the Impanda Mission till sometime the next day. We were not that far away; it just took forever. I was riding inside of the bus, but it was full, and so there were actually some people riding on top of the bus. We each brought our own food and water. Each time a herd of elephants, monkeys or giraffes would cross the road, the bus would stop for them. Maybe it would take them ten minutes, or it might take an hour for them to finish crossing. However long, we waited. In this part of Africa, the animals had the right-of-way.

Marian "Pat" Benedict Cmdr. USN NC Ret.

The Silence of the Pain is Deafening

If someone needed a restroom, he tapped the driver on the shoulder and the bus stopped and waited while one or more passengers found a bush to use. When it was time for a meal, the driver would find a place to pull over and we would all disembark and eat. We would then each find a bush to use, and then get back on the bus.

At one point, when we were bumping along on this bumpy road, all of a sudden the bus came to a halt. I don't think that the bus ever went faster than about twenty five or thirty miles per hour, so we weren't thrown when the bus stopped short like that, but it got my attention. Then the men jumped off of the bus and the women just sat there very quietly while the men ran off into the bush with sticks.

I asked the bus driver, "What are they doing?"

He said, "They are going to go get monkey meat."

The men then brought the dead monkeys back and put them on top of the bus, where some of the Africans were riding. Then the bus continued down the road.

I will never forget my first Christmas in Africa. To this day, I believe that the stars and the moon are bigger and brighter in Africa than anywhere else on God's earth. It was very hot, probably around 115 degrees. Bishop Imsekila had come up from the Chala Mission to the Impanda Mission to say midnight Mass. The Priest, the Brother, Sister Pauline, Sister

Africa: A Call to Serve and to Learn

Lilia (a nurse), Fran Laterza and I were the only white people, and the only ones who wore shoes to the midnight Mass. That midnight Mass was the first time I had stopped to consider, in the few months that I had been in Africa, that very few Africans wore shoes. There wasn't a door to the church. The confessional wasn't closed or curtained off, because of the heat and the body odor. We would kneel before the Priest and confess in the open. Families weren't seated together, because the men were always seated on the left side of the church, while the women and children were seated on the right.

It was during the Mass that the Africans there announced that they would be giving a gift to us, the missionary people. I asked myself first, why would they do that, and second, what gift could that impoverished African community give to us?

It was the most humbling, the kindest, and the most meaningful gift that I ever received; not only at Christmas, but at any other time. The Africans sang Silent Night in English for us as our Christmas gift. I cried. The moon was bright, flooding the bush with light; if that scene had been in a movie, it could not have been done better. Hollywood could not have produced something more beautiful or more meaningful than that. When I think of that night, I think: "That's why I went to Africa." That is: not just to help others, but to share in an exchange of love elsewhere in the world.

Marian "Pat" Benedict Cmdr. USN NC Ret.

The Silence of the Pain is Deafening

I had been a firm believer that God has made life simple for

us; a belief that my time in Africa reinforced. Life should be easy, as if we could just fall through it. We are the ones who complicate it all. We create our own hell here on earth. The simplicity of the African nations at that time, around 1960, was a simplicity that I wished the American people could have had. Life was simple, life was meaningful and life was beautiful and peaceful. It was the best Christmas that I have ever had.

Sister Pauline departed for Ireland in January of 1961, for a short rest. She had TB, which was being controlled; also, she had been in Africa, working at the mission for about five years. She deserved (and needed) a rest. That left Fran, Sister Lilia and myself with a forty bed hospital to manage on our own. I was scared, I was lonely, I was homesick and I had just caught something, a fever, which might have been the beginning of malaria or even something worse.

The day after Sister Pauline left, a woman, at full term in her pregnancy, came in with the baby's arm protruding from her vagina. She had spent about twelve hours in labor, while some of the African midwives tried to deliver the baby. I was scared, since Sister Pauline had been our only doctor. There was a doctor in Tobora, but the train to Tobora usually took twenty-four hours each way, even though Tobora wasn't very far from us.

I had Fran anaesthetize the woman with ether, which was safer. I was to rearrange the baby within her before delivery, a procedure which was much less likely to injure the mother if she was unconscious or nearly so at the time. I had nothing handy to tie the umbilical cord after delivery. I finally did deliver the baby. By the time delivery was complete, it had been some two and a half hours since I had last heard the fetal heartbeat. It wasn't a big surprise, then that the baby was stillborn. I used one of my shoelaces to tie off the umbilical cord. I really didn't have any alternative but to proceed as I did. Although the baby was lost, the woman, who was at risk of a fatal hemorrhage, survived in good health.

There's an old Spanish word, gana. Gana means desire or wish. Additionally, there was a movie out called Dead Poet

The Silence of the Pain is Deafening

Society, in which there was talk about Carpe Diem (Latin for *seize the day*). When I was in Africa, I felt in touch with my desires and my feelings and my ambitions and my hopes and my dreams, and I tried to seize the day every day. If I could have maintained that for the rest of my life, God knows what I might have accomplished in this world. I wish I hadn't fallen back into my old self after I returned. But: Africa! God, I loved it. It was great.

Again, while Sister Pauline was away, another woman arrived at the hospital to give birth. It was at two o'clock in the morning that an African man came pounding on the door; his wife was ready to deliver. I woke up and shook my shoes out before putting them on (we learned right away to check our shoes for scorpions and such). We were escorted to the hospital that night by one of the Africans who carried a rifle. There was word that there was a leopard in the area. I never saw the leopard, but that was the word. I remember telling the woman "hapana sacuma," do not push, do not push, do not push. She pushed. When she delivered that child, she lacerated right through the rectum. I had to send an African boy back to the house to get Fran up and to get Sister Pauline's medical book to find out how to repair a sphincter and a rectum. I had never done that before. Thankfully, I managed to sew her up right and she soon had functional bowels.

My Story

Africa: A Call to Serve and to Learn

I also delivered a woman whose husband was a Christian teacher at the elementary school in Impanda, the local town. Impanda was a one block square town set up by the British when the mines were active. It was about five miles away from the hospital. The stores in town were owned and operated by people from India. The school teacher approached the hospital, saying that his wife was beginning labor and that she was bleeding vaginally. I thought to myself, "Why don't these things happen when Sister Dr. Pauline is around?"

I noticed that after her contractions stopped, she would lose bright red blood. When her contractions began again, the bleeding would stop. Also, she had minimal pain, and so I thought that a marginal placenta praevia was likely. In this somewhat rare pregnancy complication, part of the placenta is abnormally located and breaks open. A fatal hemorrhage is possible, even likely, if nothing is done for the mother, and taking steps to prevent the hemorrhage often results in the loss of the baby. I took a special clamp and clamped it on the head of the baby. I sat with gentle pressure holding the baby's head securely against the cervix to keep the woman from bleeding too much. I sat for two or three hours, holding the clamp, keeping very gentle pressure against the cervix until she dilated completely. We asked her to push and as she delivered this infant, the placenta came out immediately. So the diagnosis was correct, that she had a partial placental praevia. We had a live baby! God does work in Africa as he does all over the world. Several days later, this family approached me and wanted me to be the godmother of their infant. I was thrilled; I was absolutely thrilled that they would ask me. The poverty was such that there were no baby clothes over there; no booties or diapers; nothing that we are used to. They just wrapped a cloth around the infant. It was such a beautiful baby. When Father baptized the child, he spoke in Latin, Kiswahili, English, French, and Dutch. It was a big thrill for me. It is a memory that I will keep forever.

We also had an autoclave in what was our operating room. The operating room was originally part of a medical clinic for a mine, an English mine that was there years ago, where the Brits mined God-knows-what. An autoclave has a high temperature, pressurized chamber which is used to sterilize equipment. We hired an African to keep the pressure lamp hot, so as to keep the temperature up high enough to sterilize the instruments to operate. We paid him 14 shillings a day, which was about two dollars. That's how we managed to get sterile instruments in our operating room.

Sister Pauline did a lot of surgery. I learned to be first assistant and to cut and tie and to hold retractors, in addition to the various other things that interns and resident doctors normally do in operating rooms in modern countries.

One thing I loved about the Africans was their sense of humor. They laughed very easily. Something minor that I might think of as somewhat humorous, they would find absolutely hilarious. I loved how easily they laughed. Another

thing I loved was the simplicity of their lifestyle. Such simplicity of life is fantastic; it envelopes an outsider with an allure of its own. When that person returns to civilization, he or she will want to try to keep that simplicity and ease of living. Over a period of time, of course, it disappears. We get caught up in the mainstream of life and hurrying and worrying, and then of course, we long for the simplicity and ease we once knew.

I am very fond of popcorn and I had asked my mother to send me some popcorn, something I missed in Africa. They had corn, called mashelly in Kiswahili, but popcorn was not known to the people where I was. One Saturday Fran and I went down to the town, where I had a package waiting. I opened it, and to my joy, there was the popcorn.

We told Fostino, the African boy who cleaned our house, and Apolonari, the cook, that this was mashelly (corn). They understood the statement, but they just kind of looked at it. We had a wooden stove, which was out on what might be called the back porch, an outdoor part of the house which was all screened in against the bugs. Fran, Fostino and I went in through the screen door. I put some popcorn in a pot with some oil and covered it with a lid. We were trying to explain the production of popcorn to this African house boy, Fostino. He would stand there and smile and say "indio, mama," which meant "yes," if he understood what we were talking about. Then he would say, "hapana," that is, "no," when he didn't understand something. All of a sudden he heard the popping going on in the pot. He stepped back. I can still see him in my mind's eye. He was smiling and then his eyes got bigger. But he kept smiling, if only a stressed, half-smile, while we gently shook the pot to keep it popping.

Fran wanted to show him what the popping noise was, so she held the pot out and raised the lid. Popcorn started flying out of the pot and Fostino made a dash through the door. When he made the dash I made a dash right behind him to grab him.

Africa: A Call to Serve and to Learn

He might never have come back– and I mean never. I stopped him long enough that he could come to terms with it all. He was frightened, yet he was half-laughing. I was trying to be serious but I couldn't help but laugh too. Fran had put the lid back on the pot. When the popping finally stopped, I brought him back inside the porch. Fran set the pot on what passed for a table. As Fran started to raise the lid, I thought he was going to dive for the door again. I thought, "God, I don't know if I can do this again." I was still a little out of breath. We were talking as best we could in Swahili to this house-boy, explaining that it was mashelly, and that you eat it. Well, that didn't go over too well. Fran finally raised the lid, and I took a piece and put it in my mouth, chewed it up and swallowed it. He looked at the popcorn, he looked at me, he looked at Fran, he looked back at the popcorn, he looked at me, and said, "indio, mama, indio." Yes, mama, yes.

Finally, after ten or fifteen minutes of working with him, we took some popcorn and placed it in his hand. He finally put some in his mouth. He didn't particularly care for it. Much, much later, when we were preparing to leave Africa, Apolonari was the one who popped the popcorn for everyone. Fostino always laughed and laughed whenever he heard the popping. He wasn't a fan of eating the stuff, but it seemed the sound was the funniest thing he had ever heard.

Marian "Pat" Benedict Cmdr. USN NC Ret.

The Silence of the Pain is Deafening

Things never really got boring in Africa. Peaceful, yes, but boring, no. One day, Fran and I were headed toward town on the old dirt road. It was a five mile trip from the hospital to the town of Impanda. It might have been Sunday Mass we were going to, I'm not sure; I remember we had our prayer books with us. The vehicle was an English car, so Fran was on the right side, behind the wheel. There weren't any American style cars there, so I had to learn to shift with my left hand. I was pretty well Africanized by this time– that is: a bit laid back, taking life in stride. Otherwise, I really don't know how I would have reacted. Maybe back in the States I would have panicked or blown a fuse or however you might say it. Anyway, we were tooling along down on this road; Fran and I were just talking away about something or other. I happened to be looking up when the left front wheel of the car came off. It rolled out ahead of us and then just rolled off to the left, into a field.

I said to Fran: "Oh, there goes the front wheel."

"OK," she replied.

Then, all of a sudden, the car just –kerplunk– stopped. Of course it stopped: we had just lost a front wheel; nothing unusual there. So we calmly continued the conversation we were having, as we set out on foot, prayer books in hand. We left the car sitting there. We didn't expect it would be stolen, not with the wheel missing. There wasn't a lot of theft, and most of the Africans didn't know how to drive anyway. So we walked on down to the Mission, where the Catholic church was, for whatever it was that we were going to do there. Father had a picky-picky. A picky-picky in Swahili is a motor scooter. He first took Fran back to the Mission on the back of the motor scooter, and then he returned to bring me.

Being well Africanized, none of us had gotten upset over the car. We thought, "Well, we will get it fixed tomorrow, or we will get it fixed some other day. If Father William can't fix it, we will have to wait till another white Father/Brother comes into town. Or maybe one of the Indians; or if we need a part, one of the Indians maybe can tell us what we need. Then we'll just wait till the day the train comes and brings the part. Or whatever."

In Africa, there aren't a lot of nervous breakdowns. There isn't much in the way of domestic violence; you wouldn't witness a lot of the yelling and screaming or the losing of tempers like we have back in the States or in Europe. Life is simple; life is kind; life is patient. Life like that is very addicting. The more time in Africa, the more patient a person becomes. If not, the impatient person would become a loner, because everybody else is very calm.

Marian "Pat" Benedict Cmdr. USN NC Ret.

The Silence of the Pain is Deafening

On the porch at the house we had a ping-pong table. It had

a net and we had some ping-pong balls, but we had no paddles. So we made our own ping-pong paddles out of cigar box lids, which were given to us by the Indians in town. Life like that is simply better.

Nowadays, when news breaks, it's on television screens all over the world in minutes. In Africa back then, we could tune into the BBC, the British Broadcasting Company. We had fifteen minutes of English news from London at night on our radio. That was it. I'll never forget it. Sometimes we would listen to it and sometimes we just weren't that interested in what was going on in the rest of the world. News wasn't something that we just had to have. The Africanized mind is comfortable not knowing what the rest of the world is doing.

Africa: A Call to Serve and to Learn

There was one time, however when we wanted to keep up with the news. My cousin Bob sent me Time magazine (he says that was the first time he ever helped me; he has *really* helped me tremendously since). Of course, by the time I got it, the magazine might have been two months (or even more) old. Our mail didn't come that often, and if the train broke down, or if the rains came so the train couldn't get through, we just didn't get any mail. So we could go weeks or even months without mail.

We found out that John Glenn, the astronaut, was to go into orbit. We must have read that in Time Magazine, because there was nothing else from the outside world to read. In fact there was nothing else to read, period. Because there was nothing else to read, I would read every word in the advertisements, the names of the publishers and the editors and the contributors; simply: I read every word I could find in the magazine. To this day, I read everything in my Newsweek and Time magazines, just out of habit.

So when we read that John Glenn was to be going into orbit, we tuned into the BBC to find out about it. We learned then that he was already up, either in orbit or on his way, or at least he was up at the time that the news story we heard was prepared. Then our fifteen minutes of news was over and we had to wait 24 hours to find out if he survived. That turned out

Marian "Pat" Benedict Cmdr. USN NC Ret.

to be a long wait. Thankfully, John Glen did survive; he spent nearly five hours in earth orbit, the first American to orbit the earth. It was all very exciting.

Our ping-pong table was built for us by Father William, for which we were grateful. Also, Fran and I would play Scrabble, then we would play Scrabble, then we played Scrabble some more. So we had some recreation during our midday break. We performed surgeries in the morning, after which the clinic was open to patients for a couple of hours. But in the afternoon, when temperatures were oppressive, none of us worked other than to make the rounds in the hospital. We had an African nurse who would do that, since she was more accustomed to the heat. But sometimes Fran or I would take turns making the rounds.

Because the midday heat was so oppressive, if there was some need of something from one of the stores in town, we would have to go early or we would have to wait, because at midday the stores would be closed. They would then open back up in the evening. But we still put in long days, despite being idle during the heat of the day. Between the operating room, the clinic, pulling teeth and delivering babies, we were kept quite busy.

I had been in Africa for quite some time when it was announced that Monsignor Browers, the founder of the Lay

Africa: A Call to Serve and to Learn

Missionary Helpers, would be coming to Tobora. There was talk that a hospital might be built, either at Impanda or at Chala. We were doing the best we could with what we had to work with, but it really wasn't a hospital from our point of view. So it boosted our spirits to think that maybe people in the United States would donate some money and someone would put up some concrete walls and get some beds with sheets and blankets and maybe there would be generators and a laundry room, and maybe even air conditioning, and we could have a decent hospital.

I had a cold, or some infection, at about that time. I remember Fran saying that maybe I needed a shot of penicillin, just in case, and I thought that sounded like a good idea. I'd had penicillin previously without complications. However, when she gave me a shot of penicillin at the clinic, I had a severe reaction.

I said, "Fran, I cannot breathe."

Fran gave me some anti-histamines, and we headed out of the hospital. When we got to the house, we hopped in the car and drove down to the Mission right away. I responded well to the anti-histamines, so by the time we got to town, I was breathing better.

We sat outside at the Mission. The sun went down, and then we sat and watched it get dark. I could breathe well by then, but I still had a rash. It was the first time I had a reaction to penicillin, and the last time as well: I've never taken any since. I looked up at the clear, star-spattered sky. It had cooled off a bit; the kerosene lights were on in the Father's house and there were a few lights at the Mission as well. I thought, "God, isn't it beautiful! It's almost paradise!"

It was all so different than how I had grown up. The Africans had never seen a tall building. For some of them, our car was the first car they had seen. Electricity, clothes, a department store, ice cream, a movie theater, airplanes; many of them had never seen an airplane, much less a jet. But I often wondered, which continent was the one better off? Even with all the technology and the speed, the hospitals and the medical research; even with all the food that we have in the United States, I could honestly sit there and wonder who really was better off.

The Africans had peace of mind and contentment. Which peoples were the ones in touch with what life is really all about? In Africa, people weren't so cluttered by material things. I don't just mean money, particularly, but material things like buildings, and garbage cans and highways; billboards, posters and advertisements; all of the things that can distract us from life itself. In Africa, we had each other.

Africa: A Call to Serve and to Learn

Millions of people walk down 5th Avenue in New York and are not even aware of the person walking next to them. Even among their closest friends, people in the States typically don't see the pain within the other person. There just isn't the required closeness among friends. In Africa, in the bush, we would see the joy and the pain and the fear; we would share in the laughter. In modern countries like the United States, what we most often see is the mask that people wear in defense of the inner self.

I have spent so much time running around, trying to be someone whom I thought other people wanted me to be. In the bush, one can be stripped of all of that and become a real human being. The bush seems to give us permission to be ourselves. In the bush, we are free to cry and to laugh, to ponder and to pray, to meditate and to see so much more. I found a peace, an inner peace in Africa that I have never had since. The full contentment and inner peace that is possible for

Marian "Pat" Benedict Cmdr. USN NC Ret.

a human to experience is not to be found in modern countries. Sometimes it's almost there, but really, it's never fully there.

I was preparing to do a gastric lavage (stomach pumping or cleaning) on a young African man. There was only one stomach tube in the hospital; I dipped it in mineral oil to aid in insertion. It went in through his nose and down into his stomach, so that I could get a sample of his stomach contents for the lab tests that Sister Pauline had ordered. I explained all this to him, and carefully inserted the tube. I then had to run out, and so I left him alone for a couple of minutes. Apparently he thought I hadn't finished inserting the tube, and that maybe I was having difficulty, because upon my return I found that he had removed the tube. He had pulled it entirely out and he had taken his machete and had cut it precisely into small, almost identical pieces. You would have thought he had a ruler, which he didn't. I patiently asked him why he did that. If it had happened here in the United States, I would have exploded, especially since the hospital was then without a stomach tube. But I was patient with the young African man.

He said, "Mama, because, when you cut it in smaller pieces, it is easier to get into the stomach." And he was right. So much easier than going up through the nose.

I didn't get mad at him; I just smiled, and he smiled. He did very well at helping in very much the wrong way, and I did very well at remaining calm, and life went on.

The Africans are beautiful people; they are intelligent, and what they do makes sense, even when what they do is completely wrong. However, beautiful, warm, loving people that they are, they do not understand the kind of routine hugging and kissing that Europeans and Americans sometimes engage in. We put our arms around people and hug them and kiss them: especially with good friends, and especially when there are strong emotions.

We had to learn, in Africa, that hugging and kissing were not done and that they wouldn't understand it. As a general rule it was to be avoided. Maybe with a young house boy, after he knew you awhile, you could be standing there talking to him and put your arm around his shoulder. But we were told not to do that. It's just not one of their customs.

There was a young boy named Mathody, with beautiful eyes, who lived near the mission at Impanda. Oh, I could have

The Silence of the Pain is Deafening

taken him home in a minute. One day, he was going into church. I had not been in Africa very long. Father William was walking in with me. Mathody was at the door. He turned around and he smiled at me. He was dressed in rags. Six years old and he had never owned a pair of pants. He smiled at me and then he began to go into the church, and so I reached over just to pat him on the bottom. The Father stopped me, asking me not to do that, which I understood once he explained it.

I was with Father William one time several months after that. Mathody used to wait at the church for me and smile when he saw me. So I commented to Father William what a precious, darling, sweet, child this was.

And Father William said, "No, he isn't." He said, "Mathody waits for you to come and then he smiles and does all that just as a show, and then he goes into the church."

But one time Mathody set out on his own, this six year old boy, and walked the five miles from Impanda to the hospital. We looked up one day and there he was at the clinic.

I said, "Mathody, what are you doing here?"

And he just kind of smiled. Sister Pauline lectured him.

She said to me, "You are going to have to put him in the car and take him back down to the mission."

So I drove him back down to the mission, because that was where his mother worked.

My Story

Africa: A Call to Serve and to Learn

I had written to my mother and my sister about Mathody. Of course, I had become very attached to him. They sent me some boy's shorts; not undershorts, but shorts. The Africans around there wouldn't know what underwear was. I took the shorts down to the mission one day and found Mathody there, with a filthy sarong wrapped around him. He had the most gorgeous eyes. I showed the pants, the little cut-off shorts to his mother. She cried; she just sobbed. She took him around to the side of the church and put the shorts on him, and brought him back around. Oh, God, I wish I had a picture. Six years on this earth and those shorts were the first clothes he had owned. I've often wondered where Mathody is today. If he remembers any of this. He was a child that I was very, very fond of.

We had a dog named Bobby. He was a black dog; just a stray dog that we fed. We were walking over to the hospital to work one morning, and there was no Bobby. We wondered where he was.

I turned around and I said, "Domoo, domoo," (blood). There was blood on the front porch. We went and got Fostino and Apolonari.

They said, "Leopard, mama, leopard!" And they became very frightened.

We thought, "Oh, my God, how could a leopard get that dog during the night and we not hear it?" Well, we didn't hear

Marian "Pat" Benedict Cmdr. USN NC Ret.

it. Later that day, they found the dog. The neck was chewed by the leopard and his back leg was almost gone. We had to kill him. Sometime later, someone in a nearby village finally killed the leopard. That was the only incident that I can recall involving a wild animal at our hospital or where we lived.

One time Fran and I were traveling to another village when the game warden stopped us on the road and said we were needed in a nearby hut. He guided us to a thatch hut, which had no windows. It was terribly hot inside, smelly and dark. There was a woman about to deliver a baby there and we had no medical bag.

I said, "My God, Fran."

I could see nothing until my eyes adjusted, and I just hoped that the baby would wait until I could see. The woman was in labor and I said, "God, Fran, I've got to deliver this baby."

I did deliver the baby. We each took a shoestring out of our shoe, and tied the cord in two places. Fran pulled a pair of scissors out of her pocket, cut the cord, and that was that. I was reminded of what my mother used to say to me: "Make do." You make do when you're in the bush.

Several weeks later a small plane brought some people over from Tobora. They were from England, and as they did from time to time, they came to work on closing down the old mine operation. It was the mine which brought about the houses

Africa: A Call to Serve and to Learn

which we turned into a hospital and a residence. Also, the mine brought about the town of Impanda, with its square block of little stores owned by folks from India.

One day one of the local men who was working with the English people shutting down the mine, was gored by a wild boar. Some of the English people brought him into the clinic with his intestines hanging out. I thought he was as good as dead, that he would soon die.

I thought, "My God, we can't fix this guy."

Sister Pauline, our surgeon, was not there. I had never seen someone with his entire intestine hanging out of him. We decided to load this guy on the plane to get him to Tobora; there was no other way he might survive. After putting sulfur on his intestines, Fran and I wrapped a sterile dressing tight around him; we gave him a penicillin shot and loaded him into the plane.

I said," My God, Fran the man's gonna die." Medical professionals can't stop everything and worry about any one particular patient. Once the patient is gone from the clinic, it's out of sight, out of mind. I thought, "Well, he'll just die, and that's the end of that."

It was maybe seven weeks later that an African guy came up to the clinic on foot. He said, "Jambo, mama." Hello, mama.

Marian "Pat" Benedict Cmdr. USN NC Ret.

The Silence of the Pain is Deafening

I looked at him and he looked at me and he smiled and he looked at Fran, and I thought, "God, who is this guy?"

He said, "Santie, sanna, mama," and he bowed and bowed and bowed. He handed us the towel that we had placed on his gut that was hanging out. He wanted to return the towel. It was clean! We had him pull up his shirt; he had a nice incision healing. He thanked us again and went back into the bush.

How do we know God's plan? How do we know who will live and who will not? Only God knows when your time is up.

The part of Africa I was in had a rainy season –roughly December through April– which made life interesting, if not challenging, for everyone. We were dependent upon the train for travel, and for supplies and mail service. One rainy season the tracks were under four feet of water, so we had to do without for a while.

As you might imagine, we would wait each year to see what the rains would do. I remember the first year wondering what all the smoke was from. It was late in the fall and there was smoke or the smell of smoke everywhere. I found out that along every road there were fires, and so I asked what was going on. It turned out that the Africans were burning the bushes and the tall grasses along the roads, ahead of the rainy season. They would burn everything along the roads so that the heavy rains wouldn't uproot the plants and wash them all over the roads, making the roads impassable. So life can be interesting in Africa.

The pace of life was slow where I was in Africa, and so I took opportunities to think, to meditate and to look within.

Ernest Cretcher once said, "There are two kinds of thinkers. Those who think alone and those who cause others to think."

I was each of those thinkers at times while in Africa. My time in Africa not only spawned intellectual growth for me, it was a spiritual growing experience as well. I like the quote, "Men run to and fro in the earth and knowledge is increased." We should always look to increase our knowledge as we run about.

St. Augustine once said that we will be restless until we rest in Him. I believe that. I was restless when I went to Africa. I was looking; I was searching, and I do the same thing today. But I have come to accept the fact that I am a restless person. Until I rest in Him, until I rest in my God, my Creator, I will have to live with my restlessness.

Life must have a purpose. If death were the end of us, then how absurd it would be that we were born in the first place. It just makes sense that there is more beyond this temporary existence. My job on earth did not end with Africa. Africa was something that was essential to my growth. I don't think of myself as a body with a soul to be saved. Rather, I'm a soul

Marian "Pat" Benedict Cmdr. USN NC Ret.

that has a body; a soul that has a temporary living quarter. I have a purpose, or really, God has a purpose for me, or I would not be here. Mysterious are the ways of Deity. We are here to do God's will. We are not here to understand it.

I had a job to do in Africa. I had the calling to go and I went. Answering my call was one of my most beautiful spiritual experiences. Because there is a God, there was a purpose for it all.

Plato said, "The soul knows all things. Learning is only recollection." I would love to go back to Africa and recollect more.

Chapter Six
The USS Repose
Naval Hospital

The Silence of the Pain is Deafening

THE SECRETARY OF THE NAVY

WASHINGTON

The secretary of the Navy takes pleasure in commending

USS REPOSE (AH -16)

For service as set forth in the following

CITATION:

For exceptionally meritorious service from 22 Feb. 1966 to 8 Feb. 1967 while providing medical facilities afloat in waters adjacent to the I Corps Tactical Zone and in primary support of the III Marine Amphibious Force, Republic of Vietnam. Providing exceptional and selfless service in pursuit of her mission to save lives and reduce suffering, USS REPOSE admitted 4,927 patients, 1,758 of which were critically injured combat casualties; performed over 2,000 surgical operations, more than 1,600 of which were classified as major surgery; and administered 3,067 pints of blood during emergency life-saving surgical and intensive care procedures. More than two-thirds of all patients were subsequently returned to duty due to the excellent treatment received. In support of the I Corps Tactical Zone, REPOSE rendered outstanding medical service during twenty-six combat operations, including DOUBLE EAGLE, UTAH, HASTINGS, COLORADO, DECKHOUSE IV, PRAIRIE AND DESOTO. While operating in waters off the Da Nang, Chu Lai, Phu Bai, and Dong Ha Tactical Areas of responsibility, REPOSE habitually averaged forty to sixty continuous days "on the line", and accepted over 3,000 helicopter landings without a mishap. In addition to combat medical support, REPOSE provided 6,200 outpatient and consultation services to Free-World Military Forces and Vietnamese civilians in urgent need of medical service and humanitarian care. She performed all combat medical support with the minute mortality rate of slightly over one percent of patients received, one of the lowest mortality rates in the annals of warfare. The outstanding dedication to duty, resourcefulness and inspiring professional skill demonstrated by the hospital staff and ship's company were in keeping with the highest traditions of the United States Naval Service.

All personnel attached to and serving on board USS REPOSE during the period designated above, or any part thereof, are hereby authorized to wear the Navy Unit Commendation Ribbon.

Secretary of the Navy

My Story

USS Repose Hospital Ship

Marian "Pat" Benedict Cmdr. USN NC Ret.

The Silence of the Pain is Deafening

NAVAL HOSPITAL
USS REPOSE (AH-16)
FPO San Francisco 96601

00:RPN:vls
1650
18 Dec 1966

From: Commanding Officer, Naval Hospital, USS REPOSE (AH-16), FPO San Francisco 96601
To: Lieutenant Commander Marian BENEDICT, NC, USN, 566708/2900
Subj: Letter of Commendation

1. On the occasion of your detachment from this command, I wish to commend you for your outstanding services rendered during the period 1 Nov 1965 to 18 Dec 1966 as set forth below:

During your tour aboard the USS REPOSE (AH-16) from the date of its reactivation to the present time, your primary duty has been that of Central Supply Supervisor. In this capacity your performance has been outstanding. You have met all the demands of your assignment with self-assurance and ease. The fact that the ship has always been sufficiently supplied with CSR items has been due to your conscientious efforts. Additionally, you have demonstrated considerable imagination and creativeness in improvising supplies not immediately available. Of special note has been your performance in the Recovery and Operating Rooms where you skillfully administered nursing care measures to causalities. Your superior knowledge and technical talents have contributed to the highest quality of professional care to each of your patients. Mass immunization programs aboard the USSREPOSE are a continuous process. You have personally coordinated and supervised the administration of all immunization programs and maintained accurate records. Your exemplary conduct as a nurse is a source of inspiration to all your associates. It is with distinct pleasure, therefore, that I award you this so richly deserved Letter of Commendation.

2. Each of your shipmates extend to you warm wishes for continued health, success and happiness in your new assignment.

3. A copy of this letter will be attached to your fitness report and made a part of your official serve record.

Rudolph P. Nadbath

My Story

USS Repose Hospital Ship

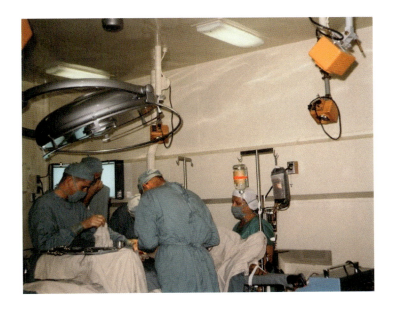

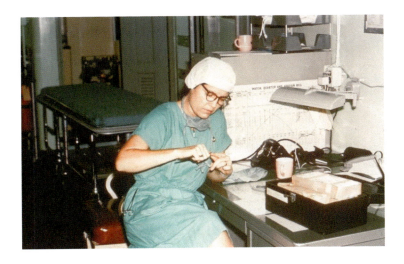

Marian "Pat" Benedict Cmdr. USN NC Ret.

Profile

Captain Maher

Commanding Officer of the USS Repose Naval Hospital

In 1927, Captain Maher joined the navy to see the world. He graduated from the Naval Academy in 1932, and went into inactive duty in the Naval Reserve. He was recalled to active duty in 1940. Captain Maher commissioned and commanded a patrol craft and two destroyer escorts; he served in both the north Atlantic and the western Pacific through WWII.

Captain Maher completed eight Arctic and two Antarctic expeditions as commanding officer. He "wintered over" in the Antarctic as commander of Antarctic Support Activities for Deep Freeze III. He completed one tour with OPNAV, as a cold weather expert, and another as an assistant inspector general in command of a frozen stores ship, supplying the sixth fleet. Captain Maher served as commander of the Naval Station at Subic Bay in the Philippines, and finally, he completed a tour as Deputy Chief of Staff for Naval Reserve, Eleventh Naval District, which brings him to his assignment as Commanding Officer of the USS Repose.

Captain Maher holds the Navy Marine Corps medal for life saving in the Antarctic plus various area campaign medals and occupation medals.

My Story

USS Repose Hospital Ship

Profile

Captain Paul R Engle, M.C. USN

Officer in Command, USS Repose Naval Hospital

Captain Engle received his MD degree from the University of Michigan in 1940 and entered the U.S. Navy in 1941, shortly before the attack on Pearl Harbor. From then he served continuously until this writing. His war time duty included a tour as medical officer aboard the USS Detroit.

Captain Engle's shore assignments included medical duty at the U.S. Naval Hospital in Bethesda, Maryland. Also, in 1948 and 49, he served as Chief of Medicine at the U.S. Naval Hospital in Guam. In 1950 he underwent post-graduate study in tropical medicine at the Tulane University School of Medicine. In 1955 and 1956 he completed the resident course at the Armed Forces Industrial College. After that he served three years as the Force Medical Officer of Service Force, also known as COMSERVPAC, which was, at the time, a service support command of the US Pacific Fleet.

From 1959 to this writing, Captain Engle has served as the Director of the Physical Qualification and Medical Records Division at the Bureau of Medicine and Surgery, Navy Department in Washington, D.C.

Marian "Pat" Benedict Cmdr. USN NC Ret.

The Silence of the Pain is Deafening

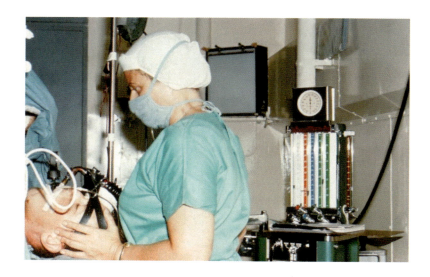

My Story

USS Repose Hospital Ship

On June 15, 1965, the Repose, affectionately nicknamed "Angel of the Orient" was being recalled to active duty. Vietnam would be her third war in the Pacific.

At Hunters Point Naval Shipyard, south of San Francisco California, an around the clock re-activation began. Shipyard workers and navy men worked 24 hours a day, all summer and into the fall of 1965.

One hundred and fifty days after she came out of retirement, Repose was once again ready to join the active fleet. She was then a modern, 750 bed, floating hospital. She had all of the latest diagnostic and treatment equipment. On October 16, 1965, she was re-commissioned and ready to go wherever needed.

She carried enough medical supplies to operate continuously for nine months. The Repose had a frozen blood bank designed to supplement rather than replace the hospital's whole blood supply, the 250 pints of frozen blood could be

> **Timeline of the USS Repose from her birth to retirement**
> (Historical Research from BU Med)
>
> 22 Oct 1943
> Construction of Repose (AH-16) was started
>
> 8 Aug 1944
> Launched
>
> 14 Sept 1944
> Placed in service
>
> 26 May 1945
> She was commissioned
>
> 8 July 1945
> Departed Norfolk, Va.
> Transited the Panama Canal
>
> 29 July 1945
> Arrived in Pearl Harbor

Marian "Pat" Benedict Cmdr. USN NC Ret.

stored indefinitely and reconstituted in minutes. She carried a new sonar echo encephalograph, which doctors could use to locate brain hemorrhages and metal fragments undetectable with x-ray equipment. Also on board was a recompression chamber if needed, used for either aviation casualties resulting from rapid loss of aircraft pressurization or diving casualties due to decompression sickness (sometimes called "the bends").

The Repose's crew consisted of 14 officers and 200 enlisted men. The ship's "second crew" or hospital staff, included 24 doctors, 29 nurses and 250 corpsmen. There were oral surgeons, dental technicians, medical service personnel and chaplains.

By Christmas of 1965, the Repose had competed her shakedown cruise from Hunter's Point to San Diego and back to San Francisco. In January of 1966 she left San Francisco for

> 7 Aug 1945
> 700 patients embarked at Pearl Harbor for transport to San Francisco
>
> 24 Aug 1945
> Scheduled to steam for Philippines via Honolulu, the Repose was diverted to Okinawa to ride out a typhoon. She arrived at Okinawa on the 15th of September
>
> 20 Sept 1945
> She operated at Shanghai as a base hospital, attached to service squadron-10 until March 10, 1946
>
> 10 March 1946
> She remained in Shanghai until October 15th of 1946
>
> 1 Nov 1946
> The Repose arrived at San Francisco for leave and upkeep

USS Repose Hospital Ship

waters off of Chu Lai, a port city in Vietnam with a Marine Corps base. She traveled by way of Pearl Harbor in Hawaii, and Subic Bay in the Philippines. There were hot meals, running water, clean linens and air conditioning (luxuries I was not prepared for!). By the time we got on line, at the end of January, the ship's crew and the Hospital crew were performing as a team.

My personal story begins with the fact that I had three corpsman in the control supply department that I was in charge of. I also took the operating room call every third night, and I worked in the operating room and triage when needed. I want to say right off we had the best corpsman God ever created, and I mean in all departments. I never witnessed any disagreements among any of the hospital personnel, doctors or nurses.

5 Feb 1947
The Repose sailed for Yokosuka, Japan

14 Feb 1947
She was moved from there to Tsingtao, China

1 March 1947
The Repose served as a base hospital through September of 1948 and then remained in Asian waters

5 July 1949
She steamed for the West Coast.

27 July 1949
The Repose arrived at Long Beach, California

September 1949
She was assigned to the San Francisco group of the Pacific Reserve fleet

28 Oct 1949
She commenced inactivation

Marian "Pat" Benedict Cmdr. USN NC Ret.

The Silence of the Pain is Deafening

There are things I have forgotten, other memories have been blocked out, but I will try to recall some of the incidents that I experienced on board the Repose.

Our first casualty was named, if I recall correctly, Mike Neely. I believe that, as of this writing, some of the nurses still keep in touch with him. He had stepped on a land mine and had lost both legs. The helicopter landed in the middle of the night, and when they lifted him off the chopper, we saw that someone (probably a field hospital corpsman) had wrapped a belt around both of his stumps to stop the bleeding. It was not unusual to put six pints of blood in a double amputee upon arrival. He was rushed first to the operating room, and then placed in intensive care.

As he stabilized, I said out loud, to no one in particular, "We are in a war."

> 19 Jan 1950
> The Repose was decommissioned and placed in reserve
>
> Korean War
>
> 20 July 1950
> The Repose was ordered activated at the earliest possible date
>
> 26 Aug 1950
> She was delivered ready, and five days later she was authorized to operate with a civilian crew
>
> 2 Sept 1950
> She sailed for Yokohama, Japan
>
> 16 Sept 1950
> She arrived in Yokohama. There a Navy crew embarked and next day she steamed for Pusan, Korea arriving 20 September

USS Repose Hospital Ship

I don't think he realized for the next few days that his legs were gone I cannot tell you how many double amputees we encountered while I was aboard that ship, but it was a lot.

Mike was eventually medevac'd to Clark Air Force Hospital in the Philippines. From there he was medevac'd to Oakland Naval Hospital in California. The Oakland Naval Hospital was an amputee center. An amputee would be held there until he could be medevac'd to a military hospital near his home. At the amputee center, patients got together with other amputees they could identify with, which helped them cope with their own loss. Coping was a grueling experience for them.

> 26 Oct 1950
> She served at Pusan as a station hospital. She departed for Yokohama with 189 patients
>
> 28 Oct 1950
> She was re-commissioned
>
> 13 Nov 1950
> She served in Korean waters at Inchon, Chinnapo and Pusan before transporting 301 patients to Yokohama, Japan
>
> 5 Feb 1951
> She underwent availability. From there Repose returned to Korea where she provided hospital services between Korean and Japanese ports
>
> 29 Jan 1952
> She departed Yokosuka, Japan for the West coast with one stop at Pearl Harbor

The Repose had an Autoclave, which is a machine with a high-temperature pressure chamber that can sterilize everything from bandages to the operating room instruments. The one we had broke down frequently, causing no end of

Marian "Pat" Benedict Cmdr. USN NC Ret.

stress and problems for me, for my crew and for the surgery crew. Time and time again, I would come to work and find that it had broken down. It was just something we all had to put up with. Finally we made a deal with the Chaplains (Catholic and Protestant). About three times a week one would come by and pray over the Autoclave.

I still hate that Autoclave, even to this day. Years later, when the Repose was sold for scrap, sad as I was that the Repose was finally retired, I thought of the Autoclave and was cheered up to think of it being scrapped. Later, when the new hospital ship, "The Sanctuary" was being readied for deployment to the South China Sea, I worried that the Autoclave from the Repose had been salvaged and installed in The Sanctuary. I told them again and again: "Get a new Autoclave!" They finally did.

> **11 Feb 1952**
> A call at San Diego was followed by overhaul and installation of a stern (rear) helicopter platform at Long Beach
>
> **23 April 1952**
> Sea trials were completed. She left San Diego, California a month later for the Far East
>
> **24 June 1952**
> The Repose arrived at Inchon Harbor, South Korea. She commenced receiving patients the same day
>
> **22 July 1952**
> She was joined by the hospital ship Haven (AH-12)
>
> **14 Feb 1953**
> After a long period of patient transfer operations between Korean and Japanese ports. The Repose steamed for San Francisco

USS Repose Hospital Ship

The one blessing we had aboard the Repose was excellent teamwork. The ship's crew and the hospital crew had a wonderful relationship. We all just did our own jobs, which is how things work best. One evening we were overwhelmed with casualties. Since we only had three operating rooms, the surgeons could only operate so fast. I kept thinking to myself, I wonder what the parents or other relatives of this patient or that patient were doing at this hour. Were they asleep? at work? shopping? eating dinner? What were they doing as this soldier was dying or that one was being operated on? I have no idea why I was thinking that. It just came to me when we were so busy. Sometimes things would just go through my mind like that.

> 6 March 1953
> The Repose arrived at San Francisco
>
> 2 April 1953
> She was transferred to Craig Shipbuilding Co. in Long Beach
>
> 12 May 1953
> She underwent repairs through 23 May. The Repose then steamed for Pearl Harbor. From there she left for Japan.
>
> 5 June 1953
> Repose arrived at Yokosuka
>
> 14 June 1953
> Repose again was stationed at Inchon Harbor and operations in Korea recommenced. She made several patient transfer runs to Japan
>
> 11 Feb 1954
> Via Pearl Harbor, she arrived in San Diego, California

The Repose, moving off shore, followed the Battles on land. Sometimes the ship had to move offline; that is: with the

Marian "Pat" Benedict Cmdr. USN NC Ret.

hospital effectively shut down. In those cases, helicopters would first take the wounded to the field hospitals at the bases on land.

> 28 April 1954-1 Sept. 1954
> She remained at Long Beach, California naval shipyard
>
> 2 Sept 1954
> She arrived in San Francisco, California
>
> 27 Sept 1954
> Repose was transferred to naval reserve fleet San Francisco group
>
> 21 Dec 1954
> She was decommissioned at Hunters Point Naval shipyard. There were many Navy people, I'm sure, who, like myself, thought that the Repose had at last found rest. But that was not to be.

It was on July 18, 1966 that 12 casualties requiring immediate surgery were received within two hours and sent directly to the operating rooms. Since we only had three operating rooms, surgeons decided who would get immediate service and who would wait. The most severe wounds got immediate attention. Within the following nine days, approximately 200 casualties were admitted. During those nine days, the highest number of casualties admitted in a 24-hour period was 72. Three operating rooms functioned continuously for five days, completing major surgery on 79 patients. I would sometimes be up for 30 hours at a time.

When we were up all night, the ship's crew made sandwiches and coffee, or served iced tea and soft drinks. Not just the food and beverages, but really: the comradery is what gave us the boost we needed to keep going.

In this particular instance, unlike previous casualties, the majority of injuries were due to sniper fire and typically included abdominal and chest wounds. Other wounds were due to multiple shrapnel fragments, sometimes necessitating several surgical procedures on the same patient. The full gamut of technical equipment from chest pumps to respirators, to hypothermia blankets and decompression chambers was employed during this period.

One night, as the helicopters full of wounded soldiers were lined up to land, one of the corpsman who was top side to help unload the wounded, told me later that night that one helicopter almost missed the landing area. He though, "My God! He is going over the side!"

> **Vietnam: her third and final war**
>
> After 10 ½ years with the reserve fleet at Suisun Bay, California, the Repose was activated and towed to the. Bethlehem Steel shipyard. The weary ol' gal had one last mission to accomplish. On June 19, 1965, she was brought to Hunter's Point Naval shipyard. On Oct 16, 1965, the Repose was re-commissioned at Hunter's point. Captain Eugene H. Maher was in command and Captain Paul R. Engle, M.C., was the senior medical officer. It was there that we became friends.
>
> 3 Jan 1966
> The Repose departed from San Francisco. She arrived at Pearl Harbor, Hawaii on the 9th of January, 1966.
> 3 Feb 1966
> The Repose arrived Subic Bay, Philippines for supplies and some repairs

Marian "Pat" Benedict Cmdr. USN NC Ret.

The Silence of the Pain is Deafening

The pilot then made another approach and landed perfectly. We found out later that the pilot was so tired he had started to doze off. There is no timetable to the killing and wounding of life in war.

At times when things were quiet, we would go top side. The China Sea was often quiet, except for a few oriental sampan boats, each with one or two Vietnamese sailors guiding it. One day I asked the captain of the ship what if those sampans had explosives on board and the sailors wanted to blow up our ship? He just smiled and said "If they did we would never know, would we?" I had to think about that for a while. I'm sure the captain knew what was in those sampans. On a quiet night, when the sky was clear, off in the distance I could hear the ammunition exploding, and frequently, I could see the flashes and flares light up the sky.

> 14 Feb 1966
> She sailed for Vietnam, arrived online and commenced medical support at Chu Lai. Indeed she lived up to her nickname "Angel of the Orient". The Repose was permanently deployed to South East Asia. The 721-Bed floating hospital operated mainly in the I-Corps area which include Da Nang, Chu Lai, Phu Bai, Dong Ha, and Quang Tru.
>
> After serving in Southeast Asian waters, where she treated more than 9,000 battle casualties, and admitted over 24,000 patients for inpatient care, on March 14, 1970, the Repose departed from Vietnam for the United States. The repose was there decommissioned and placed in reserve in May of 1970.

My Story

USS Repose Hospital Ship

At times (not often), when casualty loads decreased we took children aboard. Some had harelips which we repaired, others had fever, dysentery, vomiting; some were malnourished. The parents would just leave them with us. Of course, everyone fell in love with them. One of the young boys, one about 10 years old, had some minor surgery. When he felt better he helped me and my corpsmen fold bandages. He was really kind of a funny boy. And then these delightful children all went back to a war zone.

I have prayed for all our troops, regardless of what war. When I think of the wars we had in the Middle East, I think: "My God, what a waste of human life!" One time we had a Marine on a gurney and I washed his face, and I was cleaning his finger nails when someone walked past me.

As he passed by he said, "Pat, he is dead."

> The U.S. Navy commission pennant for a hospital ship is the Red Cross. After the commission pennant was lowered, the hospital ship was no longer the responsibility of the commanding officer. The commanding officer of the USS Repose (AH-16), Captain Robert F. Menge, USN, received the commission pennant.
>
> In August of 1970, as is traditional, the ensign was presented to the Senior Petty Officer. And then, to the crew member with the longest service on board, the 'Union Jack' was presented to S.A. Gardner.
>
> After the 15th of August 1970 she served another five years in reserve as a dockside hospital for the Long Beach, California Naval hospital. After more than 20 years commissioned service spanning three wars "The Angel of the Orient" was finished.

Marian "Pat" Benedict Cmdr. USN NC Ret.

The Silence of the Pain is Deafening

I knew that. I said, "I don't want his mother to see him this way."

In the morgues at Da Nang they completely prepare the body before it goes into the casket to be sent back to the United States. I knew that too, but sometimes in the midst of pain and death, my mind would just float around, and what I felt like doing wasn't always logical.

USS Repose Hospital Ship

Typical Surgery Log
USS Repose, Naval Hospital
Emergency Surgery Added to Schedule for Wednesday, October 12, 1966

C4   Left Thoracotomy, Suture Repair Lacerated Left Carotid Artery, Tracheostomy, W/D (Wound Dressing) Both Legs and Drainage of Scrotum

C6   Exploratory Laparotomy, Excision Meckel's Diverticulum, Splenectomy, and Appendectomy

C3   Exploratory Laparotomy, Suture Repair Laceration Liver, Appendectomy, W/D Left Arm, and Lower Leg, End to End Anastomosis, Brachial Artery, Arteriogram

B1   W/D Right Arm, End to End Anastomosis Brachial Artery, Arteriogram

Marian "Pat" Benedict Cmdr. USN NC Ret.

The Silence of the Pain is Deafening

Surgery Schedule for Friday October 14, 1966

Room I

B6 Mitral Commissurotomy, Probable Valve Replacement

C3 Repair Ventricular Septal Defect

Room II

C6 W/D and Dressing Change Right Anterior Thigh

Emergency Surgery Added to Schedule for Friday, October 14, 1966

C3 W/D Right Thigh, Removal Foreign Body Right Thigh, End to End Anastomosis Right Popliteal Artery

C6 W/D Both Legs, Right Thigh, Vein Graft to Right Femoral Artery

B1 W/D and Fasciotomy Left Arm

C6 W/D Right Lower Leg

My Story

USS Repose Hospital Ship

C4	Tracheostomy, Exploration of Left Neck, Removal Bullet From Carotid Bifurcation, Right Antrostomy with Debridement and Packing, Exploration Right Pterygoid Space, Ligation, Right External Carotid, W/D Both Legs
SOQ	W/D Right Arm
C4	Arthrotomy, Left Knee, W/D Both Legs Orchiectomy
C4	Exploratory Laparotomy Suture Repair Laceration Liver, W/D Both Legs And both Arms, W/D Scalp, Right Frontal Craniotomy Right Frontal Craniectomy
B6	Right Frontal Craniotomy

Marian "Pat" Benedict Cmdr. USN NC Ret.

The Silence of the Pain is Deafening

Surgery Schedule for Monday, October 17, 1966

174

Ward	Operation

Room I

C3　Delayed Primary Wound Closure Left Arm, Left Leg

C3　Delayed Primary Wound Closure Both Legs

C3　Delayed Primary Wound Closures Both Arms and Right Leg

Room III

B1　W/D (Wound Dressing) Both Legs

B1　W/D and Delayed Primary Wound Closure Right Arm

Room II

SOQ　W/D, Dressing Change and Delayed primary Wound Closure Right Arm

My Story

USS Repose Hospital Ship

Where are you my brothers?

Are you in the wind?

…sometimes near; often pushing against me…

do not push me away

for I am here…

(perhaps I need to let go)

Marian "Pat" Benedict Cmdr. USN NC Ret.

The Silence of the Pain is Deafening

Are you in the clouds?
…on warm, clear days I see your face…
the face of pain
on the days it rains, it's like human blood
the blood you spilled on such an empty war

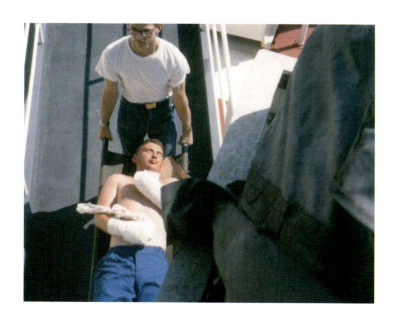

My Story

USS Repose Hospital Ship

Where are you my brothers?
…with your souls so pure and white and clean…
your lives became dirty like the mud in a jungle
in a foreign country which held no joy
only wounds and pain and death

Marian "Pat" Benedict Cmdr. USN NC Ret.

The Silence of the Pain is Deafening

Where are you my brothers?
…in a no man's land that is really every man's land…
we were all trying to build bridges to tomorrow
but you did not live to touch our tomorrows

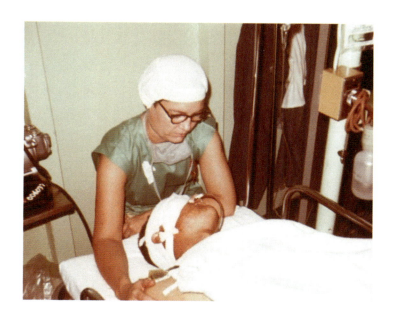

My Story

USS Repose Hospital Ship

Where are you my brothers?
did you feel the pain of failure?
…it is superficial and fleeting…
…it comes quickly and will soon be forgotten…
but for those of us who lived
the pain of sorrow
begins deep inside
growing until it consumes us

Pat Benedict CDR NC USN Ret

Marian "Pat" Benedict Cmdr. USN NC Ret.

The Silence of the Pain is Deafening

Nurse's Notes from USS Repose

The following is based on excerpts taken from communiques received from the USS Repose during July and August of 1966

During July the Repose went to Subic Bay in the Philippines to replenish fuel and supplies. On July 15, 1966, she departed for Vietnam. On the 17th of July, the Repose arrived on station off the coast of Hue-Phu-Bai. There, General Lewis W. Walt, USMC came on board to brief the hospital staff on "Operation Hastings," so that the ship could follow, in the water, the battles on land. The next day, July 18th, we were overwhelmed with casualties; we received 12 casualties requiring immediate surgery in two hours on that day and about 200 more during the following nine days, as mentioned on page 166 above.

In August 1966, we were on station for almost the entire month. The ship covered I Corps from Da Nang up to Dong Ha. From time to time, the casualties would be massive, depending on the amount of action ashore. We came to expect more casualties at night, when the enemy was usually more active.

Heart Surgery

We were proud to have been the first hospital ship to perform open heart surgery at sea and in a war zone. During surgery the female patient was on the portable heart and lung machine for a total pump time of 19 minutes. She was in Intensive Care for four days, then transferred to the International Ward for two months. She did really well. A few days her surgery, we received five Vietnamese civilians who were injured in the bombing of a village restaurant. They arrived simultaneously and they all required craniotomies (surgical opening of the skull).

Stormy Night

It was on a night with severely injured soldiers in all three operating rooms that a fierce storm suddenly rose up in the South China Sea. With the ship tilting side to side as it was being tossed up and down, we needed some extra hands. We called topside for some corpsmen from the ship's crew to come down (as if they had nothing else to do) and hold the IV poles and the overhead lights steady so that surgery could continue. The oxygen and other compressed gas tanks were also a problem; with the ship being tossed in every different direction, what wasn't bolted down needed to be steadied. Helicopters were being directed to army surgical hospitals on land, since the Repose was just too erratic for a landing. It seemed as though the night would never end, but it finally did, and everyone made it through, including the surgery patients.

Marian "Pat" Benedict Cmdr. USN NC Ret.

The Silence of the Pain is Deafening

One Big Team

One time we were operating for some 50 days without being resupplied. This was another time that the ship's crew was called on to help us– in this case it was their blood that was needed. The enlisted men's chow hall was converted to a blood donating center and the entire crew– medical and nautical– came to donate. The atmosphere there was lively; it was a wonderful feeling having everyone come together to help. Finally we went off line and headed for Subic Bay in the Philippines for supplies and some much needed rest.

No Time for Pins

After we returned to the war zone there was a day when there were some 10 patients in the triage area (where decisions were made about who should be helped first). The corpsmen and I were working there, cutting clothes off of wounded soldiers, when I saw a grenade taped to the chest of one unconscious soldier. I also saw that the grenade didn't have its pin, so that if the handle were released from the tape, the grenade would explode some seconds later. I sounded the alarm (that is: I screamed for security) and someone from security brought a pin to put in the grenade. He then took it topside and threw it out into the sea.

My Story

USS Repose Hospital Ship

I went to visit the soldier in the recovery area a few days later; he was to be medevacked to a hospital closer to his home. I finally asked him about the grenade. It seemed a good question at the time: why would someone have a grenade with no pin taped to their chest?

He evidently thought I was a bit slow. He explained that if one needed a grenade on short notice, it saved time if the pin didn't have to be pulled. He then asked for a hug before he left, and I said, "Absolutely!" I think he was glad I noticed that the pin wasn't in the grenade.

Chaplin Friend

I first boarded the Repose at Hunter's Point, just south of San Francisco, Calif. We got underway, and our first stop on the way to Vietnam was Pearl Harbor in Hawaii, where I met a Navy Catholic Chaplain, Father Cain. We became friends and had dinner together before I left.

It was maybe a year later; I was busy on board the Repose. A handful of casualties had recently arrived, and I was helping to prepare some for surgery. I heard someone call my name several times and I went over there. It was Father Cain. He had been assigned to a unit on the ground. He had crawled out to help a wounded Marine and was shot by a sniper. I was only able to talk with him briefly before he was brought in for

The Silence of the Pain is Deafening

surgery. The bullet had left him paralyzed from the waist down. I didn't see him again on board the Repose.

It wasn't until a few months later that I heard that he had been moved to the VA hospital at Long Beach, Calif. A few months after that I was done in Vietnam; I received orders to report to the Naval Hospital in San Diego, Calif., where I was to work in OR.

An aunt of mine lived near the VA hospital in Long Beach, and so, when I went to visit her one weekend, I took the opportunity to go see how Father Cain was doing.

When I walked into his room at the hospital there, he looked up and asked, "Pat?"

I said, "Yes, it's me."

He spoke strongly: "Get out of here!"

I had no idea what the problem was, but I left right away. A few weeks later, he contacted me and asked me to come visit him again. I was confused, but I went.

I found his room at the VA hospital and when I went in he started to cry, and then he started to apologize. I hugged him and told him there was no need for an apology. He told me that seeing me brought back the memories of the war, and of the Repose. He evidently was having great difficulty coping with his loss.

USS Repose Hospital Ship

We talked for a little while, and then Father Cain told me why he had asked me to come. He asked me to pull his footlocker out from under the bed and to remove his uniforms and shoes. He asked that I find someone to give them to. Of course I did. We hugged again and that was the last I saw of him. I don't know where he finally ended up, but I still think of him now and again.

Mystery Marine

Years after I had last seen Father Cain, I pulled my own footlocker out and went through it. In one of the pockets of an old green OR uniform, I found a dog tag:

> Barnes
> T.M.
> 219-74-85-49-0
> USMC M
> Bapt.

I checked everywhere I could think of: USMC in Washington DC, the Veterans of America, Marine Corps headquarters, Social Security, the Red Cross, the Vietnam Memorial Wall and the Repose patient list. There is no record of this soldier. I still carry the dog tag around, for reasons I can't explain. Perhaps in the next life he and I will meet…

The USS Repose, Angel of the Orient, has her secrets; she's been scrapped, but her secrets live on. What I would say to her today is, "Well done."

Marian "Pat" Benedict Cmdr. USN NC Ret.

The Silence of the Pain is Deafening

I must tell you about one Vietnamese boy. His name was Lip and he was eight years old. Lip was an orphan and he was blind from cataracts. After his corneal transplants, he stayed aboard the Repose for over three months. I must say he did very well; he gained some eyesight, but most of all he received a lot of love.

She always lived up to her name
"Angel of the Orient"

My Story

USS Repose Hospital Ship

Pat wrote this at the time. What changes we've seen! —ed.

Navy Nurses

Seventeen women: fourteen of them were Navy Nurses; there were two American Red Cross workers and one Navy Medical Corps Officer. They shared, with 630 men, the USS Repose, a 521 foot long, floating naval hospital.

The South China Sea was picturesque. With quiet waters and expansive skies, the moonlit nights were enchantingly romantic. However, romance was not what brought these women to the Vietnam war zone. These professional women were driven by a desire to help people, and a war zone was one place where there would be plenty of people needing medical help.

The Chief Nurse was Commander Angelica Vitillo. She served at a Navy Hospital on Guam during World War II. As she once put it, the biggest problem in a war zone is keeping the medical crew from working themselves to death. The motivation for medical professionals in war can be all-consuming, so although these 17 women were all single, romance was not foremost on their minds.

More than half of the men aboard the vessel were hospital technicians and doctors who were accustomed to working alongside women. But for most of the 300 sailors, whose job it was to keep the ship afloat, this was a new experience.

Marian "Pat" Benedict Cmdr. USN NC Ret.

The Silence of the Pain is Deafening

Tactfully, tacitly in fact, the women aboard the Repose influenced the sailors. And they were in fact influenced: not only did they reform their salty language, but indeed, observers noted more courtesy among the crew members than what might be found on board an all-male ship.

There were two areas which were off limits to men: a sun bathing area above the main deck and the nurse's quarters, located behind a grey door marked "Nurse Country". The nurses, who grew in number to 29, were housed in 16 double state rooms, except for Commander Vitillo, who enjoyed a single state room. To help compensate for the cramped living space, the Navy relaxed its regulations and allowed the women to decorate their rooms. Some of the rooms came to look like little college dorm rooms. The women shared a community shower and laundry room with a washing machine and an ironing board. They also shared what came to be their prized possession: a tiny, but fully equipped, beauty parlor, stocked with cosmetics which were donated by two large American manufactures.

It was, for most of them, a new life, but one they wouldn't trade. They were where they wanted to be: in a war zone, caring for our military.

My Story

USS Repose Hospital Ship

Edited lecture notes from a course Pat took —ed.

The US Navy Blood Bank
Blood Freezing Program

Since the discovery of blood groups in 1900 by Karl Landsteiner, the transfusing of human blood has advanced from a haphazard art to a lifesaving science. The division of donor blood into four blood groups was step one. Matching donor blood types to patients, or cross-matching, which was first done in 1907 by Ottenberg of the Rockefeller Institute in New York, was step two. The biggest problem, from that point on, has been keeping blood ready and in suitable condition for transfusion. This was a particular problem in wartime, when the donors would often be far from those in desperate need of their blood.

Blood tends to clot soon after it is removed from the human body and blood clots can be fatal to the patient receiving the blood. Thus began the efforts to have clot-free blood made available when and where needed.

One of the first solutions to the clotting problem was proposed in 1914 by Dr. Turner, then of the Rockefeller Institute. He and one of his associates at the institute, Oswald Hope Robinson, developed the idea of using a large vat of recently donated blood. As surgery progressed, blood which was slower to clot was separated out for use. In America his

Marian "Pat" Benedict Cmdr. USN NC Ret.

idea was considered impractical. In Britton, however, his ideas were accepted. He and his ideas were put to use in Flanders field in 1918. He later became head of the Pierce Co. Blood Bank in Tacoma, Washington.

From this impractical start the American military has maintained a keen interest in the development of blood banks, and in particular, in lengthening the storage time of blood. A Navy-trained tech, working with the Army and Baxter Medical worked out the Baxter vacuum bottle. This started, in 1937, the first Plasma bank, which was at the Peter Brent Brigham Hospital in Boston. Later he worked with the Miami Blood bank, making typing serums.

By World War II, blood plasma came to be the 1st choice for shock resuscitation. However, the doctors on the front lines cried out for whole blood, not just plasma, for their wounded patients, and eventually they got it through organized blood banks. It was during the Second World War that the Navy began to use Acid-Citrate-Dextrose as a solution to the blood clotting problem in the Pacific Theatre.

Following World War II, ACD (Acid-Citrate-Dextrose) was the established anti blood-clotting solution. During the Korean Conflict, locally produced blood plasma was a great spreader of hepatitis, while whole blood, treated with ACD, could be used in the field after being air-lifted from the States. Thus ACD became the standard.

In the years since, little improvement has been made beyond the ACD solution. Several other mechanisms have been used either to reduce platelet loss (EDTA sol) or to lower the potassium (resin exchange bag) with limited acceptance. In the Boston area a CPD solution was thought to be the great answer, keeping blood for 30 days. Then some side effect occurred and it was taken off the market. This left only ACD, which could keep blood for up to 21 days.

For logistic reasons the Navy became interested in freezing blood cells. The great problem in freezing blood is that crystals of ice pierce the cell walls. Through a method of using glycerol in salt solutions, small quantities of cells could be frozen, with a nominal success rate. This technique was acceptable for blood samples stored for use in the lab, but not for transfusion purposes, because a good portion of the cells were lost in reconstitution. Also, blood cells can be fast frozen in liquid nitrogen, to be later warmed in a saline solution, which was, once again, adequate for small aliquots of blood for laboratory use, but not for large volumes of blood. The liquid nitrogen itself presented problems, since it must be transported and kept in thickly insulated (thus large) containers, which few blood banks were set up to store or make use of.

Marian "Pat" Benedict Cmdr. USN NC Ret.

Quite a bit of experimental work was done by the Red Cross in Washington D.C. and by Dr. Merryman of NMRI, NNMC in Bethesda, Maryland. For example, Dr. Merryman tried shell drying of blood cells into small pellets to be stored at room temperature. This system seemed to hold some promise, but it was never brought to feasibility for transfusions.

Until 1963, freezing in glycerin by the Cone method (named after Dr. Cone) was the only functioning method for long term blood storage. However, it was an impractical method. The volume produced at the Blood Research Lab in Chelsea, Mass. was quite low, and laborious hours followed to re-sterilize all of the parts which would be reused. There were also difficulties involving the material to be used for re-suspension. Much of what was said and written against the frozen blood programs at that time were against the re-constitution methods and materials, rather than against the freezing of blood itself.

As stated, the basic problem in freezing blood is that red blood cells, which are shaped somewhat like Lifesaver candies, contain fluid inside their shell walls. This fluid freezes, forming small sharp crystals, which can pierce the cell wall, destroying the cell (called hemolysis). Lovelock, in 1953, showed that if the liquid was replaced, the cells would not burst on freezing. Using the principle of osmosis, a heavy inert substance such as glycerol or DMSO (dimethylsulfoxide) or propylene glycol would replace the fluid inside the cell. These heavy inert substances are called endocellular cryophylactic agents, or ECA's. The various types of ECA's are designed to protect the cells from bursting during freezing. Then, during post-thaw, the protective agent is washed out and the cell remains whole and viable.

Beginning in 1953, at the Blood Research Lab in Chelsea, Mass, research involving a glycerin ECA progressed. The blood was reconstituted in its own plasma and 5% albumin. The process took about 1 hour, and the volume produced at the lab was at that time about 8 units per day. Since then, Dr. Charles E. Huggins made good progress in improving the yield when reconstituting frozen blood by using dextrose and other sugars to clump the blood cells together in solution during the post-thaw wash.

The Navy's Frozen Blood Banks as of this writing are as follows:

1. Blood Research Lab. at USNH Chelsea, Mass
2. Mobile Frozen Blood Bank Da Nang, South Vietnam
3. US Navy Hospital ships (the Repose and others)

Marian "Pat" Benedict Cmdr. USN NC Ret.

Chapter Seven

Vietnam:

A Brief History

The Silence of the Pain is Deafening

From memory, documents and articles

Why am I including this in an autobiography? Most of the sacrifices of war, particularly of wars involving America, are forgotten with time. Typically, in most history classes, the gory details of America's involvement in a war are not taught. What it took to earn and maintain our freedom can be glossed over in our minds. But not in my mind.

I have been all over the world and I have not found a country I would rather live in. The Vietnam War involved me personally and so it has indelibly impressed on my mind the reality of war, even though that particular war, I believe, had nothing to do with our freedoms. (You may find this chapter of my autobiography sharply honest).

What do we say to the Vietnam veteran? What do we say to those who are missing legs, arms or eyesight? What do we say to those who are still out there, perhaps captured or otherwise MIA (missing in action)? And if we could speak to those who died, if we could read the names on the Vietnam Memorial Wall and then speak to each person, one by one, what would we say?

I doubt that very many people today think about the Vietnam war; even those old enough to remember it.

My Story

Vietnam: A Brief History

While I will never forget, I now can find peace within, in part because over time I have learned to forgive all of the lies from our politicians in Washington.

If some are looking for vindication, or for a reason for all of the suffering, they will not find it. Most of the politicians themselves were probably not looking for reasons or even for answers; if they were looking for answers, then they were not asking the right questions.

The Vietnam War to me was a wasting of my country's soul. Had we learned more from it, perhaps it would have been less of a waste. But looking back in history, I don't think we learn much from the sufferings of war. Vietnam was also an unwanted war for most Americans. And for those of us still suffering, it remains a war that will not end.

"Did I create emotional blindness?" asked Robert McNamara, our Secretary of Defense at that time.

McNamara, after some 57,000 American deaths and immeasurable bloodshed, said, "We were wrong, terribly wrong."

Really now, Mr. Secretary. And how do we explain that to the families of those who were killed and of those who are still missing?

Many of us tried to shut the war out of our minds, but this silenced our hearts, making us insensitive to some of our own

Marian "Pat" Benedict Cmdr. USN NC Ret.

feelings. To the Americans, to the South Vietnamese and especially to the children, Vietnam was a crumbling of souls. In that protracted war, what we created was corruption and more corruption. Since we humans repeat so many of our mistakes, maybe we are born in our fellow man's pain only to die in our own pain. Man's inhumanity to man runs against the laws of our Creator; perhaps that explains why "the silence of the pain is deafening."

A Boy without a Name

Days, weeks and sometimes even months go by and I never think of him. Then suddenly there he is in the thoughts of my mind. Can I see him? Oh yes: an arm and leg blown off, a gaping hole in his chest and a severely damaged eye.

When they announced over the loud speaker on the naval hospital ship, "Stand by to receive casualties," I was eating supper in the officer's mess hall above the operating rooms. The operating rooms were located on the lower deck because the ship is steadier there, as the ship tilts back and forth.

I flew down the ladder and turned the corner, where I slid in blood. The doctors began putting chest tubes in the boy and we prepared him as quickly as possible for the operating room. They had already typed and cross-matched him for blood. Then I noticed that during all of this the boy was still conscious. How he lived in that condition for two days, I

Vietnam: A Brief History

cannot explain. And after all these years I can see him in my mind's eye, yet I have no name for him. Of all the casualties and death and body bags I saw, he stands out, for reasons I don't know.

But usually the deaths affected me more than the surviving wounded. When a patient died I wondered what his family was doing at that very moment. I also wondered if, when the family was notified of his death, they wondered who was with their son when he died.

The war in Vietnam was such a tragedy and so unnecessary. It was also a terrible loss of hope for the Vietnamese people.

President Lyndon B. Johnson was frustrated, angry and bewildered. The different branches of the Armed Forces were fighting among themselves. As for the Congress, well I was just too busy to try to figure out what they were thinking. They and the rest of the political gang in Washington had no clue how to stop the killing.

Our hospital ship, The Repose, was equipped to handle 750 patients or, if need be, up to 920 patients. The staff included 54 officers, 29 nurses, 32 Chief Petty Officers and 511 enlisted men, plus 24 doctors and 246 corpsmen. They were all donors as well their other duties, since we often ran out of blood.

Helicopter ambulances landed on and took off from the rear flight deck day and night.

Marian "Pat" Benedict Cmdr. USN NC Ret.

The Silence of the Pain is Deafening

Our blood bank kept blood at minus 85 degrees centigrade, yet it could be thawed and made ready for transfusion in 20 minutes. The fluorescent antibody microscope in the laboratory could diagnose tuberculosis in a couple of hours instead of 2 to 3 days. The pharmacy could make as much as 15 gallons of nearly any desired medical compound on short notice. The Baylor-Beall heart-lung machines were the top technology at that time and always ready for service.

There were 3 operating rooms, 8 beds in the recovery room, a hyperbaric oxygen chamber; an eye, ear, nose and throat clinic; there was a dental surgery unit, an optical department (which had a stock of 52,000 pairs of eyeglass lenses), as well as an x-ray unit and a physical therapy department.

To get the USS Repose ready for Vietnam cost 7 billion dollars (which, adjusted for inflation, would be about 50 billion today).

But with all of the above, some patients did not survive. I especially want to mention the following patient, one who did not survive. I went to the Vietnam Memorial Wall in Washington D. C. and secured a tracing of his name, which is framed and on the wall in my den.

"Peter S. Connor SSgt. U.S.M.C. Co.F, 2nd BN., 3rd Marines. On February 25, 1966, in Vietnam, while leading his platoon in an area of extensive caves and tunnels in Quang

My Story

Vietnam: A Brief History

Ngai providence, SSgt. Connor maneuvered his men forward against intermittent small arms fire. He spotted an enemy spider hole about 15 meters to his front. Connor pulled the pin from a fragmentation grenade intending to charge the hole and drop it into its depths. But, when he pulled the pin he found the firing mechanism was faulty and the fuse charge was already activated.

With only seconds to decide, (he knew he couldn't race the distance to the hole, nor could he just throw the grenade without endangering his men,) with utter disregard for his own safety, he held the grenade against himself and was mortally wounded in absorbing the terrific explosion." –*Navy Times*

He died aboard the USS Repose. He received the Congressional Medal of Honor posthumously.

I am unable to write of all the casualties as there were so many. Time has passed; some I have blocked out; nonetheless they were all very dear to me.

The Many Faces of War Shows a Broken Humanity

Have you ever tasted loneliness? If you take the time to look into the faces of Vietnam War Veterans, men and women, that is where you will find it. For many it was a war that was

Marian "Pat" Benedict Cmdr. USN NC Ret.

The Silence of the Pain is Deafening

fought within and it just does not go away. Wherever we go the pain is still there.

By writing this chapter maybe I am trying to change on the inside, to live better on the outside.

Vietnam:

a place without hope

a place of hard decisions and of many errors

- ✓ To send in US advisors
- ✓ To NOT send in US advisors
- ✓ To send in US troops
- ✓ To NOT send in troops
- ✓ To really get the US into war
- ✓ To NOT get the US in this war
- ✓ To send US military into Laos
- ✓ To NOT get our military involved in Laos
- ✓ To again and again increase US troops in South Vietnam
- ✓ To NOT increase US troops
- ✓ To increase US Bombing of North Vietnam
- ✓ To NOT increase US bombing of North Vietnam
- ✓ To begin using Agent Orange on North Vietnam
- ✓ To NOT use Agent Orange on North Vietnam

My Story

Vietnam: A Brief History

No one asked the American people whether they wanted to engage in a lengthy war of attrition on the other side of the planet. This was probably the biggest error.

Early Casualties

The first recorded casualty was Richard B. Fitzgibbon, Jr. of North Weymouth, Mass. His son, Marine Corps Lance Cpl Richard B. Fitzgibbon III was also killed, some 11 years later.

Tech Sgt. Richard B. Fitzgibbon, Jr. was a member of MAAG, Military Assistance Advisory Group. He was murdered by another US airman, June 8, 1956. His son, Marine Lance Cpl. Richard B. Fitzgibbon III was killed in action in Quant Tin, South Vietnam on September 7th, 1965. They are one of two confirmed father/son pairs to die in the War.

On board the USS Constellation, Navy pilot Everett Alvarez was briefed for a bombing mission. At the same time, shortly before midnight EDT on August 4th, 1964, President Lyndon Johnson was addressing a national television audience from the White House. A few hours earlier Alvarez had flown above a chaotic situation in the gulf of Tonkin; a situation which led to Johnson's speech. A few hours later he was shot down on his mission over Hanoi. He was the first US aviator taken captive. He would ultimately be the second-longest-held

Marian "Pat" Benedict Cmdr. USN NC Ret.

The Silence of the Pain is Deafening

POW, surviving nine years of solitary confinement and torture before his release February 12th, 1973.

His being shot down began air strikes against North Vietnam ordered by President Johnson. "I found out a few years ago," Alvarez told Vietnam Magazine, "from an air intelligence guy that on the day before, some surveillance photos had been taken that did show all of the air defenses, but instead of the photos coming directly to the ship they went to Washington first. I said: you know, that figures." Had he been aware of the air defenses, he may not have been shot down and the war might have progressed differently. When his aircraft was hit, he parachuted and hit the water (of course: no survival radio), he was captured and taken to Hanoi. He said that the only thing he told them about the USS Constellation was that he ran the popcorn machine.

Long before Alvarez there were several US military killed. Lt. Col. A. Peter Dewey, killed September 26th, 1945, in the aftermath of WWII. He was a member of the Office of Strategic Services (OSS); he was searching for missing US pilots. His last message was that South Vietnam was burning and the French and British were finished. He was gunned down on his way to Saigon airport. His body was never recovered.

My Story

Vietnam: A Brief History

Pilot James B. McGovern, Jr. and co-pilot Wallace Buford were also killed early on. McGovern was a former World War II ace and worked for the civil air transport secretly run by the CIA. They were attempting to resupply a besieged French garrison at Dien Bien Phu when they were hit by ground fire. Their plane crashed into a hillside in Laos on May 6th, 1954. McGovern's remains were recovered from an unmarked grave in Laos in 2002 and identified in 2006. He is buried in Arlington National Cemetery. The crash killed both men though Buford's remains have not been found.

Capt. Harry G. Cramer Jr. died on October 21st 1957. He was already a wounded combat veteran of the Korean War. He led a team of Green Berets who were training South Vietnamese soldiers. He was killed in an explosion near Nha Trang. The army labeled it a training accident but his comrades claimed that his death was caused by Viet Cong mortar rounds.

Maj. Dale R. Buis and Mast Sgt Chester Movnand were killed July 8th 1959. Six guerrillas struck the MAAG (Military Assistance Advisory Group) compound in Bien Hop north of Saigon, shooting Buis and Movnand as they watched a movie on a home projector.

Specialist Fourth Class James T. Davis was killed December 22nd, 1961. He was assigned to the 3rd Radio

Research unit at Tan Son Nhut Air Base. Davis was killed in a Viet Cong ambush near the old French garrison of Cau Xang. President Johnson later called Davis "the first American to fall in the defense of our freedom in Vietnam." Historians clarify that he was the first official battlefield fatality. (There was so much lying and denying by the politicians in Washington at that time that we can't always be sure of the details of the early combat deaths.)

In the Veterans of Foreign Wars (VFW) Magazine, it was reported that Green Beret Spec 5 James Gabriel Jr. was KIA (Killed in Action) April 8th, 1962 and was awarded the Bronze Star for Valor in Vietnam more than two years before the Gulf of Tonkin Resolution in 1964. Congress passed the resolution on Aug. 7 and it was enacted on the 10th. That resolution officiated our combat involvement.

War Data

The Vietnam War has been called America's longest running war, although there is some difficulty determining the start of the war, since for one thing, war was never actually declared. If our recorded history is correct, however, the longest American war was one which was fought between American Indians and various forces, starting with English colonists, then with American settlers and finally with US soldiers The war extended from April 26th, 1607, to October

Vietnam: A Brief History

5th, 1898, that is: for 291 years (although the United States of America didn't exist for the first 170 of those years).

According to the Veterans of Foreign Wars, The Cold War began on August 25th, 1945 in China and it lasted until March 12 1991, when a GI was killed by communist terrorists in Greece. That's about 46 years. The VFW says that The Cold War claimed 382 American lives in hostile action, although one could argue that the Cold War wasn't an actual war. By comparison, in Vietnam, by 1964, the US Killed in Action count was only 247. Of course, that was before the introduction of US ground combat units.

In March 1946 France recognized Ho Chi Minh's Democratic Republic of Vietnam but The First Indochina War had already begun by then. The First Indochina War is recorded as having lasted from 1946 until 1954. American intervention in Vietnam grew out of the First Indochina War.

Mistakes in Vietnam Began in the Fifties

The Vietnam War was a tragic story of good intentions paving a road to hell. President Eisenhower offered aid in exchange for reforms, and that policy continued through the Kennedy and Johnson administrations. Billions were given out but reforms weren't put in place. America seemed to have unlimited optimism about our adopted protégé. America, through our patriotic imaginings, envisioned a Southeast Asia

Marian "Pat" Benedict Cmdr. USN NC Ret.

wishing to be like us. We ignored the early signs of a developing civil war, to be fought with guerilla tactics, which according to Bernard B. Fall, the author of Vietnam Witness 1953-1966, were quite evident in the mid 1950's. As General Maxwell Taylor said in retrospect, we failed to know our friends and our enemies before entering into the conflict.

Our Southeast Asia policy was one of lost opportunities and of suppressed facts about peace negotiations. We might have otherwise avoided much bloodshed. U Thant, the Secretary General of the UN 1961-1971, told a press conference on February 24th, 1965, "I am sure that the great American people, if they only knew the true facts and the background to the developments in South Vietnam, would agree with me that further bloodshed is unnecessary." I ask why the American people didn't know the true facts.

Gulf of Tonkin Incident(s)

Original incident: August 2 1964; alleged second incident: August 4, two days later. This second incident, or alleged incident, began our escalated ground combat campaign.

Lloyd R. Joe Vasey, in the American Legion Magazine (June 2013, page 50), in a commentary entitled *"An attack took place"* makes an argument that there was a second attack in the Gulf of Tonkin on August 4, 1964. He was a Navy Rear

Vietnam: A Brief History

Admiral and at the time was chief of staff for Vice Adm. Roy Johnson, commander of the US 7th Fleet.

There has been, over the years, and still is today, a lot of confusion concerning the North Vietnamese torpedo boat attacks on the USS Maddox. Robert McNamara testified before the Senate that the USS Maddox was, at the time of the second incident, some 130 miles to the southeast of where it was said to have taken place, and had not yet begun its patrol. Most everyone agrees that the original ambush on August 2 occurred.

An internal National Security Agency historical study was declassified in 2005. While it affirmed the August 2 incident, it concluded that there were no North Vietnamese Naval vessels near the Maddox on August 4. The study reported that "Despite the Navy's claim" that two enemy torpedo boats had been sunk, there was no physical evidence, such as wreckage or bodies to support the claim. According to Lloyd R. Joe Vasey, that finding ignored the reports of the men who were there.

Did President Johnson deliberately mislead Congress and the American public in order to start a war? Or was he misled? The evidence suggests that the various players were acting in good faith at the time, with the possible exception of our president, Lyndon Johnson.

Marian "Pat" Benedict Cmdr. USN NC Ret.

The Silence of the Pain is Deafening

In the dark of night, in rough seas, on board the Maddox, sailors received radar, sonar and radio signals which they thought indicated that North Vietnamese Naval vessels were preparing for another attack like the one two days earlier. For about four hours the Maddox maneuvered and fired at targets which their radar indicated were there.

While President Johnson accurately passed on to Congress what he had been told happened, he did tell Congress that the first incident, the August 2 incident, was unprovoked, even though he knew that the Maddox was providing intelligence support to the South Vietnamese Army for attacks against the North, and was thus a legitimate target. Later, reflecting on the second incident, the August 4 incident, Johnson was quoted as saying privately, "For all I know, our navy was shooting at whales out there."

In response to news of the second attack, Congress effectively gave President Johnson the authority to wage war without a declaration of war, bypassing the American people and their constitution. The Gulf of Tonkin incident was a turning point in the Vietnam War, and whether or not the second attack was a phantom will remain a mystery. However, I am convinced that in response to the news of the attack, we should have pulled out, and left the matters in Vietnam to those who were living there.

My Story

Vietnam: A Brief History

Khe Sanh, 1967

Using information taken from articles, books and other sources, I will attempt to outline the details of what was one of Vietnam's longest battles, and one of the costliest. Hopefully anyone who reads this will realize the sacrifice our American troops made.

An American military compound was located 3 kilometers northeast of Khe Sanh (kā sän). Khe Sanh was a village located 18 miles south of the DMZ at the northern border and 8 miles east of Laos. It was centered along Route 9, which ran eastward from a coastal port, across northern South Vietnam, to the Ho Chi Minh Trail in Laos. The main purpose of this American military compound was to form a base from which to launch attacks to stop supplies moving along Route 9 from the port to the Ho Chi Minh Trail, which was the main supply route for the North Vietnam Army (NVA). The base was also there to protect Khe Sanh, the local political seat in that less-populated area near the enemy border.

Army Special Forces constructed the Khe Sanh Combat Base in 1962. During 1966, NVA infiltration down into the north end of South Vietnam grew, threatening the village of Khe Sanh. In 1967, General W. Westmoreland had the air strip extended and sent in two battalions from the 2nd and 26th Marines. The base was to be defended at all costs as

Marian "Pat" Benedict Cmdr. USN NC Ret.

The Silence of the Pain is Deafening

Westmoreland also planned to use it for clandestine operations into Laos (of all places).

On Halloween night, 1967, at midnight, the North launched a ground assault against Khe Sanh, perhaps testing our resolve. In response, Air Force F-100 fighter bombers pounded the outskirts of the compound.

The attack —or siege— of Khe Sanh began several months later on January 21, 1968. The 6,000 Marines stationed at the base were surround by three divisions of North Vietnamese fighters, totaling some 20,000 men. They were subjected to heavy and nearly continuous rocket, mortar and artillery bombardment, as well as infantry attacks against outlying positions. The Americans responded in kind; additionally they used aerial bombardment. However, bombing sorties became risky and resupply of the base became very difficult, since it was then surrounded and since aircraft was subject to intense antiaircraft fire.

Then, suddenly, on January 31st, 1968, the battle for Khe Sanh was overshadowed by the launch of the countrywide Tet Offensive (described below). General W. Westmoreland believed that one purpose of the Tet Offensive was to distract attention from Khe Sanh, and so his focus remained there. However, the fighting at Khe Sanh waned somewhat during the Tet Offensive, leading others to believe that the siege of

Vietnam: A Brief History

Khe Sanh was in part meant to distract attention from the buildup leading to the Tet Offensive. In retrospect, there may not have been any such strategic link between the two attacks; the North was simply more capable than we thought.

A few weeks later, on February 20th, intensified fighting resumed at Khe Sanh. Marine patrols were ambushed with high casualty rates, as the North Vietnamese had constructed an elaborate tunnel and bunker system almost all the way around Khe Sanh. The battle for Khe Sanh continued until April 8.

Resupply was accomplished using innovative techniques, including "Super Gaggles" of aircraft which consisted of multiple fighter-bombers surrounding a large number of helicopters, and the use of C-130 "Hercules" cargo helicopters, utilizing the high-speed LAPES delivery method.

During the battle, the US dropped a total of 5 tons of bombs and fired 8 artillery shells for each enemy combatant, according to the estimate of 20,000 enemy combatants. It was the largest aerial bombardment of the war. Was defending Khe Sanh worth all of that? The base and village might seem remote and inconsequential; however, being centered between a port and the Ho Chi Minh Trail, it was of great value to the North. In 1973 when the US pulled out of Khe Sanh, the Viet

Marian "Pat" Benedict Cmdr. USN NC Ret.

Cong occupied the base, and then later used it in the successful invasion of South Vietnam.

The Tet Offensive

Based in part upon an article in Vietnam Magazine 2013 by Mike D. Shepherd, and upon online sources.

The main offensive was from the Vietnamese New Year's Eve until the end of February (essentially four weeks' time). However, the fighting which began with the Tet Offensive continued for most of 1968, as the North continued to occupy and defend some of their original conquests. The term "Tet" referred to the Vietnamese New Year. In 1968 the usual holiday truce at the end of January was cancelled at the last minute. On the 31st of January, 80,000 North Vietnamese fighters hit 36 of 44 provincial capitals and 72 district towns in coordinated surprise attacks throughout the country. In the first few days, the North was successful, having attacked, and in some cases taken over, military and civilian command and control centers throughout South Vietnam, most notably in Saigon. However, the belief that the South Vietnamese people would then rise up against the foreign aggressors, welcome the North and call for a cease-fire, turned out to be mistaken. The North had overestimated their sympathizers amongst the South Vietnamese people.

Vietnam: A Brief History

While it was eventually a military defeat for the North, they scored a great psychological victory, over both the South Vietnamese people and the American public. It was previously assumed that the North could not launch a significant offensive, having been dealt previous defeats, being greatly outnumbered and being ill-supplied and disorganized. The battle at Khe Sanh and the Tet Offensive called into doubt information provided by the military to the US government and to the American people, and the two battles served to further weaken the American public's wartime resolve.

The death figures from the first 60 days of the Tet Offensive were staggering: from the attackers, some 58,400 North Vietnam Army and Viet Cong died; from the defenders, 4,954 South Vietnam solders, 3,895 American soldiers and 214 South Korean soldiers died; 14,300 South Vietnamese civilians also died.

Napalm

Napalm is a volatile fuel mixture with a sticky, gel-like consistency which makes it adhere to surfaces. It explodes easily and can ignite upon impact without an ignition source. The surfaces where it sticks are heated to 2200° Fahrenheit as it burns. When it sticks to human skin it often burns down to the bone.

Marian "Pat" Benedict Cmdr. USN NC Ret.

The Silence of the Pain is Deafening

Louis Fieser was Professor Emeritus at Harvard. His research included the chemical causes of cancer, vitamin K and blood clotting agents, as well as anti-malarial drugs.

In 1943: he invented napalm. He and his Harvard chemists beat the chemists from DuPont and Standard Oil in a government competition to develop an incendiary weapon. Dr. Fieser never apologized for his invention and he refused to debate the Vietnam War.

Napalm was used in WWII to fire-bomb Japanese cities. More recently the UN General Assembly adopted a treaty that defined the use of napalm or other incendiary weapons in areas with concentrations of civilians as a war crime.

In 1945 napalm bombs were dropped on Dresden, Germany, in a series of raids on the night of March 9 and into the morning of March 10. During that night 16 square miles were destroyed, 87,000 residents were killed, 100,000 were injured and 475,000 were left homeless. Similarly, during the night of March 12-13, the port city of Osaka, Japan was destroyed.

During the Vietnam War, God only knows how much napalm was dropped. We dropped countless bombs, yet after all the destruction, North Vietnam won the war.

Vietnam: A Brief History

Agent Orange

Agent Orange was the nickname given to a toxic herbicide, which could be identified by the orange stripe on its containers. This poison was sprayed on fields and towns to remove vegetation in which the enemy could hide. The results for humans include prostate cancer, respiratory cancer, soft tissue sarcoma, non-Hodgkin's lymphoma, Hodgkin's disease, chronic lymphocytic leukemia, multiple myeloma and other diseases. It is also believed to cause birth defects like Spina Bifida.

Agent Orange is still active in the Southeast Asian environment. It was sprayed heavily in Saigon, Gen Hoa, Cu Chi and Tay Ninh. The debate of whether to use Agent Orange in Vietnam started with the Kennedy administration in 1961. He was concerned both about its effectiveness and with cold war political fallout.

After all the back and forth fighting about whether to use Agent Orange in particular, and chemical warfare in general, it was settled and Agent Orange was used widely, and often indiscriminately. Even the Repose, the US hospital ship I was on, was in Agent Orange range, as I was notified, in 2013, by mail (I was in Vietnam in 1965). Perhaps the mail was a bit slow.

Marian "Pat" Benedict Cmdr. USN NC Ret.

Final Fiasco
the fall of South Vietnam

Based on online sources and on an article which appeared in Vietnam Magazine, February 2013.

The Paris Peace Accords brought about a cease-fire which existed in name only. Saigon began to push against the Vietcong and then, according to the memoirs of Tran Van Tra, the Vietcong's top commander, in March of 1973, a plan was hatched in Hanoi to take control of the country. For the next two years repairs would be made to the Ho Chi Minh Trail and elsewhere to facilitate the movement of troops and supplies. Then, during the 1975 dry season, the North would invade.

During his 1973 confirmation hearings, Secretary of Defense Schlesinger stated his opinion that America should resume bombing in the event of an invasion by the North into South Vietnam. The US Congress passed a resolution forbidding such intervention.

Starting in late December of 1974 and into early January, a few months prior to the planned invasion, the North Vietnamese Army attacked Phuoc Long Province and took the provincial capital. They waited to see if the US would resume bombing. When we did not, the plan for the invasion of South Vietnam was solidified. It began in earnest in March of 1975.

My Story

Vietnam: A Brief History

In April of 1975, two decades after the CIA engineered the birth of the Republic of Vietnam, which launched America's longest, and certainly the most controversial war, the end was quickly approaching. The Arab Oil Embargo caused fuel shortages and high prices, and had sent South Vietnam into recession, along with much of the western world. The steady reduction in US troops over the previous five years also hurt their economy, further reducing what South Vietnam could spend on war. The South Vietnamese military greatly outnumbered the North in equipment, but without sufficient fuel to operate it, there was no advantage. Meanwhile, the North Vietnamese Army was being funded and fueled by Eastern Bloc nations, which were not so affected by the embargo.

General Nguyen Van Thieu struggled to hold South Vietnam against the invasion from the North. The situation became dire, and then hopeless. After the fall of Phuoc Long, General Thieu had realized the United States would not be coming to the rescue of South Vietnam. The North Vietnamese leaders, as well, were confident of this and were also aware of the reduction in supplies from the US. They used their forces to cut off other avenues of supply to the South Vietnamese Army.

Marian "Pat" Benedict Cmdr. USN NC Ret.

The Silence of the Pain is Deafening

On April 5th of 1975, President Ford was in Palm Springs, California to play golf during the Easter Holiday. He was there briefed by Secretary of State Henry Kissinger and Army Chief of Staff General Frederick C. Weyand. The President was told that the government of South Vietnam was on the brink of defeat, and that it was time to prepare for a mass evacuation. There were some 6,000 American citizens, tens of thousands of South Vietnamese, and many people from other nations who needed evacuation. Of the Vietnamese citizens who were evacuated or who self-evacuated during that time 138,869 were processed into the US; most of the rest remained closer to home.

President Ford ordered General Fred Weyand, Army Chief of Staff and former Commander of the Military Assistance Command Vietnam (MACV), to go to Saigon and assess the situation. Some on the ground argued for more military aid for the South Vietnamese; some argued for more financial aid, more fuel and more ammunition. With or without aid, most officials agreed that the situation in Vietnam had shifted in favor of the North. General Weyand asked for 722 million in emergency aid.

Many US generals had voiced their opinion that there were no other options except for the Americans to leave. Secretary of State Henry Kissinger pushed for financial aid to South

Vietnam: A Brief History

Vietnam, at least for appearances sake, in the interest of American foreign policy. President Ford requested the $722 million which General Weyand had called for, but the Congress only authorized $250 million.

The CIA reported that some 150,000 South Vietnamese soldiers in the northern half of the country had been annihilated or had simply disappeared in the weeks since March 25th of that year, and that the North Vietnamese had captured more than a billion US dollars' worth of equipment including 400 airplanes and helicopters.

Meanwhile the powers in Washington were trying to decide how best to get out of Vietnam. It was our Ambassador in Saigon who wanted to delay the evacuation until the last minute, thinking that the South Vietnamese Army could hold Saigon and that a political solution would be found. Evacuations therefore began quietly, and in moderation, to avoid the appearance of our abandoning Saigon.

President Ford pressured Congress to amend immigration laws so that South Vietnamese citizens (to whom the US owed much) could immediately enter the United States.

On the 21st of April, the South Vietnamese President, General Nguyen Van Thieu, resigned, saying that he was misled into signing the Paris Peace Accords, being assured that the US would resume bombing of the North if they broke the

Marian "Pat" Benedict Cmdr. USN NC Ret.

ceasefire. He had first asked for more military aid and was denied. The president's resignation greatly increased the crowds arriving at the embassy for evacuation. About 40 commercial flights per day left Tan Son Nhut airport for the US base in the Philippines, until Philippine president Marcos restricted arrivals. Other US bases were then sought.

Between the 18th and the 24th of April, the US Navy assembled a multitude of ships off of Vung Tau. Movement and transport groups under the Command of the flagship USS Blue Ridge, included the USS Okinawa, USS Vancouver, USS Thomaston, USS Peoria, USS Dubuque, USS Fredrick, USS Anchorage, USS Denver, USS Duluth, USS Mobile; also: the carriers USS Hancock and the USS Midway, each carrying helicopters. Additionally, for military support and air cover, under the Seventh Fleet flagship USS Oklahoma City: USS Mount Vernon, USS Barbour County, USS Tuscaloosa, USS Worden, USS Richard B Anderson USS Cochrane, USS Kirk, USS Gurke, USS Rowan, USS Cook, USS Bausell. Also the carriers USS Enterprise and the USS Coral Sea. A dozen or so smaller vessels were on hand to help the self-evacuees at sea, and for similar rescue functions.

On the 25th of April, General Thieu and his family were taken to Taiwan on an Air Force jet. Evacuations of some

Vietnam: A Brief History

American and other foreign-national embassy staff and their families began.

President Ford continued to voice his concern about American pride. He blamed Congress for the loss of the Vietnam War.

On the 29th and 30th of April, the American military commenced a massive helicopter evacuation from Saigon, while the tactically astute North waited outside of the city. At around 11:00 am on the 30th the North Vietnamese entered the South Vietnamese Presidential Palace in Saigon. They found General Duong Van Minh and Prime Minister Vu. The General and the Prime Minister said they were willing to hand over power. The North Vietnamese responded: "You cannot handover what you no longer have."

That was the end of the Republic of Vietnam, slightly less than twenty years after the CIA had created it.

Had the American public been informed and then allowed an input when all this started, perhaps there would not have been a war at all. We might have thought that the CIA shouldn't mess around down there.

Marian "Pat" Benedict Cmdr. USN NC Ret.

The Silence of the Pain is Deafening

The Saigon Airlift
Operation "Frequent Wind"
April 29th - 30th 1975

During the fixed-wing portion of the evacuation, 50,493 people, including some 2,678 Vietnamese orphans, were flown out from the Tan Son Nhut airport. Then, on April 28, the North Vietnamese bombed the airport.

On April 29th, Operation Frequent Wind, the largest helicopter evacuation in history, commenced. During the operation, Marine helicopter pilots flew 682 trips, accumulating 1,054 flight hours. As the refugees were flown to the aircraft carriers, South Vietnamese pilots also flew helicopters out to sea in the hope that the Americans would allow them to land on their ships. Many had no pre-flight communication and not enough fuel to make it back to shore. Seeing the foreign helicopters nearing the carrier, the captain of the Midway ordered his crew to push overboard US helicopters on the flight deck to make room for the Vietnamese. Some 45 of our Huey's were dumped into the South China Sea. Many South Vietnamese pilots ditched their own helicopters at sea; having dropped off passengers, they flew off and then bailed out, hoping to be rescued at sea. Four carriers participated in Frequent Wind: the Midway, the Hancock, the Coral Sea and the Enterprise.

My Story

Vietnam: A Brief History

Vital Statistics

81 Helicopters

4 Aircraft carriers

1 Marine landing ship

1,373 Americans evacuated

5,595 South Vietnamese and other nationals evacuated

To those involved: Well Done

                                        Pat Benedict CDR NC USN Ret

Marian "Pat" Benedict Cmdr. USN NC Ret.

The Silence of the Pain is Deafening

The Vietnam Memorial Wall
aka The Wall

It was around the mid 1990's, about 30 years after I served in Vietnam that I went to The Wall with my cousin Bob. I wanted to leave a helmet there to honor one of my corpsmen who was killed in action. I also just wanted to be there and see it, and I wanted to look up some people; I wanted to experience The Wall, and maybe find some bit of closure regarding some of the deaths which had so moved me during my time in Vietnam.

I found Peter M. Connor, for instance. He was a patient on board the USS Repose. I talked to him several times and then one day he just turned his head to the side and died. A few years later he received the Congressional Medal of Honor. I placed a sheet of paper over his name and rubbed a pencil across it to form a kind of imprint. I did the same with Gerald M. Vetrano.

There were many others, of course. I saw countless deaths, but some are blocked out of my memory (too painful) and others– well, at times it was just so busy– I don't remember names, or at least last names, so I wasn't able to find them. There was one young African American man (as of 2010, of the 58,267 men listed, 33,103 were 18 years old at death, 8,283 were 19; so, yes: a *young* afro-man); this one young man was

My Story

Vietnam: A Brief History

in surgery three times before he died. I wish I could have remembered his name to find him on The Wall. Despite his condition, he had a sense of humor: each time he went for surgery, he would say, "Have Miss Katie come put me to sleep." (Katie Coptic was our anesthetist).

When I brought the helmet to lay it down for a corpsman, a security officer approached and advised that it would likely be stolen if I left it there. He suggested that I leave it with him and he would see to it that the helmet would wind up at the Smithsonian. Part of the Vietnam exhibit at the Smithsonian Museum there is a display of items left at The Wall.

I am very glad I visited The Wall, as difficult as it was for me. I kissed The Wall when I arrived and I kissed it again just before I left. I'm glad I went, but I won't return. I did what I needed to do. Also: it was a grieving experience which brought back some painful memories. Once is enough.

As I mentioned above, 33,103 were 18 years old at death, 8,283 were 19. Also, 12 soldiers were 17, 5 were 16 and one soldier, PFC Dan Bullock, was 15 years old when he died in Vietnam. 997 soldiers were killed on their first day of duty in Vietnam 1,448 soldiers were killed on their last day of duty in Vietnam; that is: the day before they would have prepared to leave. Eight women are named on The Wall; they were killed while nursing the wounded. During the Vietnam War, 244

Marian "Pat" Benedict Cmdr. USN NC Ret.

soldiers were awarded the Congressional Medal of Honor. 153 of those 244 are listed on the wall. Thirty one families lost two sons; that is: in thirty one cases two brothers were killed in that entirely needless and senseless war. Shame on the stupid and lying politicians who perpetuated that fiasco.

The Vietnam Veterans Memorial

(of which The wall is a part) is a 3-acre national memorial in Washington, DC. It is maintained by the National Park Service to honor members of the U.S. armed forces who fought in the Vietnam War. As of this writing there are three parts to the national memorial: The Wall (which honors those killed, captured or otherwise missing in action), the Three Servicemen Memorial (a statue described below) and the Vietnam Women's Memorial (which includes yours truly).

The Wall is in two sections, about 250 feet long each, etched with the names of the servicemen being honored. The Wall was designed so that a visitor sees his or her own reflection along with the names. The idea was to bring the past and present together.

The wall originally listed 58,191 names; as of May 2014, there are exactly 58,300 names, including 8 women. About 1,200 of those are listed as missing rather than killed. There are directories nearby to help people find who they are looking for. The names are classified as KIA (Killed in Action) or as

MIA (Missing in Action). A diamond identifies those who died; a cross identifies those missing. When one who was classified as missing is later determined to have died, a diamond is put over the cross. If anyone listed as missing ever did return alive, (something which had not occurred as of September 2015) his cross is to be circumscribed by a circle.

Photo by Jim Jeffery

The Three Servicemen

Near The Wall is another Vietnam memorial, a bronze statue named *The Three Servicemen* (sometimes called The Three Soldiers) by Frederick Hart. The statue depicts three soldiers: a European American, an African American and a Hispanic American. The three appear to be looking solemnly at the names of their fallen comrades on The Wall. The distance between the statue and The Wall was a design compromise: The Three Servicemen were to be looking at the names without distracting attention from The Wall.

Women's Memorial

The Vietnam Women's Memorial, a statue showing three uniformed women with a wounded soldier, is dedicated to the US women who served in the Vietnam War (most of whom were nurses). It is part of the Vietnam Veterans Memorial, and it is also located near The Wall.

There was a contest, and originally, in Glenna Goodacre's winning design, one of the uniformed women (nurses) was holding a Vietnamese baby. She didn't mean to make a political statement, but the judges later decided it might be taken as such, so they asked her to re-submit. She then changed the baby-holding nurse to one kneeling and holding an empty helmet. The Vietnam Women's Memorial was dedicated on November 11, 1993.

In Memory

Memorial Plaque

The Plaque is a 3 foot by 2 foot carved block of black granite, upon which is inscribed:

"In memory of the men and women who served in the Vietnam War and later died as a result of their service. We honor and remember their sacrifice."

My Story

Vietnam: A Brief History

Ruth Coder Fitzgerald founded The Vietnam War 'In Memory Memorial Plaque' Project. She had to struggle against opposition for years to have the In Memory Memorial Plaque completed. The main issue was that some of those who "*later died as a result of their service*" died because their government failed them in one sense or another. This would include suicide victims, those who died after exposure to Agent Orange and others who were inadequately cared for by the VA hospitals and patient services. Opposition did not come from the many veterans groups who supplied much of the private funding, nor from congress, where the bill to establish the memorial passed both houses without a single contrary vote.

Once the memorial plaque was completed and installed, the project Ms. Fitzgerald founded was discontinued, but the website for it remains, being maintained by the Vietnam War Project at Texas Tech University.

The Memorial Plaque was dedicated on November 10, 2004. It is located near The Three Servicemen statue

History

On April 27, 1979, four years after the Fall of Saigon, The Vietnam Veterans Memorial Fund (VVMF), a non-profit organization, was incorporated to produce a Vietnam veterans'

Marian "Pat" Benedict Cmdr. USN NC Ret.

memorial. A wounded Vietnam veteran, Jan Scruggs, (inspired by the film The Deer Hunter), was instrumental in the formation of the fund. With help from fellow Vietnam veterans, such as retired Navy chaplain Arnold Resnicoff, private donations totaling $8.4 million were gathered.

Congressional authorization for the construction of the memorial came a year later. The location chosen was the site of a demolished World War I Munitions Building near the Lincoln Memorial. After it was announced that the winner of a design competition would receive $50,000, 2,573 people registered for the design competition. By March 30, 1981, 1,421 designs had been submitted. A selection committee then narrowed them down; first to 232 entries to be seriously considered, then to 39 entries, from which, finally, the design by Maya Lin was selected and submitted for formal approval.

Building the Memorial

On March 11, 1982, Maya Lin's revised design was formally approved, and on March 26, 1982, ground was officially broken. The especially reflective stones for the wall came from Bangalore in India. Stone cutting and fabrication was done in Barre, Vermont. The typesetting of the original list of names was done by Datalantic in Atlanta, Georgia. The stones were then shipped to Memphis, Tennessee where the names were etched, a process which involved masking around the letters and then sandblasting.

The memorial was dedicated on November 13, 1982, after a march to its site by thousands of Vietnam War veterans. About two years later the Three Soldiers statue was dedicated.

Vietnam Veterans Memorial Collection

Some visitors leave items (as I did) at the Memorial Wall. Perishables such as flowers are discarded, and American flags in good condition are redistributed. But other items have been collected by park employees, and then catalogued and stored in the Memorial Collection. From 1992 to 2003, there was an exhibit at the Smithsonian of selected items from the collection. One such item was the Medal of Honor of Charles Liteky, which he renounced by placing the medal at the memorial in an envelope addressed to then-President Ronald Reagan.

Marian "Pat" Benedict Cmdr. USN NC Ret.

Chapter Eight

Alcoholism:

My Prison

Within My Soul

The Silence of the Pain is Deafening

It has been said, "Men hate what they have done
and women hate what they have become."
It has also been said that history turns on small things,
and so do people's lives.

My name is Pat Benedict and I am an alcoholic.

*T*hat statement took me many hard years to make. It was very difficult to admit to my alcoholism. I got sober in December of 1972 and I have remained so, as of this writing (2009), 36 years. In AA terminology, my AA birthday is December 22, 1972 and I am now 36. Think: *life begins anew when drinking stops.*

Nothing in life is to be feared, but rather understood. Once I understood that I have the disease of alcoholism, my life began to slowly fall into place and I began to live more comfortably in this world.

To my knowledge there was no alcoholism on my father's side of the family; I don't recall ever seeing him take a drink. There was, however, alcoholism on my mother's side of the family. Of the ten children in my mother's family –six girls and four boys– two of the girls were alcoholics and all but one of the boys drank heavily; in fact, one of the boys died from

My Story

Alcoholism: My Prison Within My Soul

drinking. This helped convince me that those who say that alcoholism can be genetic or hereditary are correct.

I knew what alcoholism did to people. Watching as a child, I saw the destructive effects of drinking in the behavior of the people in my family. I told myself then that I would never end up like that. But I did.

I don't remember my first drink, but I remember my first drunk: bootleg whisky out of the bottle and beer for a chaser. As described in chapter 4, page 91, above, I was a nursing student and I got super drunk and then terribly sick. I went to work in obstetrics the next day, horribly hung over. My sister came in with a pregnancy complication and nearly died. The boy was stillborn. I swore I'd never drink again, and I rarely did. I did not get drunk again for several years.

But I eventually started having an occasional drink. I liked what alcohol did for me. I could change the world in five minutes with a drink. I could come out of myself and play in this new world. I was no longer lonely. I could become part of a group –rather than feeling separated from others– or really, I could become part of life itself.

I don't recall ever having just one drink. One drink just didn't do it for me. I asked a friend one time if she ever got drunk. She said she didn't like losing control. When I got drunk I felt like I gained control.

Marian "Pat" Benedict Cmdr. USN NC Ret.

The Silence of the Pain is Deafening

It was many years later, when I was a Navy nurse, stationed at the National Navy Medical Center in Bethesda, Md., that my drinking began in earnest and my alcoholism developed. I lived in the Bethesda Officer's Quarters, where there was a vending machine which sold beer for a quarter a can.

It was there that I built up a tolerance for alcohol, so that I needed more and more to get the desired effect. I would have a few beers before going out to eat with the other nurses, so that I could get by on one or two drinks with dinner, which was usually all that they had. Even so, I felt like I never had enough.

In 1965 I was ordered to the Hospital Ship Repose, which was docked at Hunter's Point, just south of San Francisco, California. Before we left for Vietnam, I and several other nurses went ashore to have some drinks. Looking back, I can't imagine what we might have been celebrating; but at the time, we didn't imagine what we faced. The other nurses had two or three drinks; I had five or six.

We stopped in Hawaii for a couple of days, but I didn't drink. Nor did I drink at our next stop, Subic Bay in the Philippines. There was serious work ahead and I didn't want to be an embarrassment. However, while stationed in Vietnam, I did sneak some alcohol on board and I snuck an occasional drink. That is something I am not proud of.

My Story

Alcoholism: My Prison Within My Soul

After fifteen months on the Repose in Vietnam, I was ordered to report for duty at the Navy hospital in San Diego, California. I was flown to Travis Air Force Base in California, where my cousin and childhood friend Bob picked me up and drove me to Palo Alto (south of San Francisco), where he lived with his wife, Helen. A couple of days later, Helen drove me to San Francisco airport at about five in the morning. I was to catch an early flight to San Diego. I was walking to the gate with a couple of marines who had also just returned from Vietnam, the three of us in uniform, when we were accosted by some anti-war demonstrators. They were loud and aggressive; they actually cornered us against a wall. But the two marines just took it all in stride; I went along with them, as if we didn't care what the demonstrators said or did. Afterwards the three of us went to the bar to do some drinking, and so we all missed our flight. But after a few drinks we didn't really care about that either.

Once in San Diego, I began to become depressed. People there would talk about sports, politics or the weather, or whatever else, but I had been to Vietnam. I had nothing in common with anyone who hadn't been there. I had seen so much death and mutilation; I had dealt with so much trauma and drama. I had lost friends in Vietnam; I also lost about thirty

Marian "Pat" Benedict Cmdr. USN NC Ret.

pounds. With no one around in San Diego whom I could really relate to, I began to drink alone.

I began to realize that I drank too much, although I didn't always admit that to myself (denial is characteristic of alcoholism). I eventually found a drinking partner: the chief of anesthesia. He would come by my apartment in the evenings and we really drank. He lived about three blocks away and one night he got lost going back home. I knew his wife and kids. His wife didn't care where he did his drinking. One night he fell and knocked a brick loose from my fireplace with his head. At the time I was more worried about the brick that about his head. Looking back now I can see how heavy drinking distorts one's sensibilities.

I was hung over on many occasions at the hospital in San Diego. Often I would be shaking and vomiting. Once they admitted me to the hospital, thinking I had a bad gall bladder. When they would send me to the doctor because I seemed so ill, I would go to a doctor whom I knew had drinking problems of his own, so he wouldn't confront me about mine.

After I spent three years in San Diego, I was ordered to report for duty at the Navy hospital in Newport, Rhode Island. Those years in San Diego were really crazy times, so in a way I was glad to be given orders, but I did not look forward to Newport.

Alcoholism: My Prison Within My Soul

I asked my mother to fly out to see me before I left. Driving her back to Oklahoma, I stopped to use the bathroom and snuck a drink from a bottle in my purse. My mother and I had a wild argument about my drinking before I left Oklahoma City for Newport.

Traveling from Oklahoma, I dreaded my arrival in Newport, Rhode Island. I had spent nearly a year in Los Angeles before spending three years in Africa's tropical heat, I had then spent about a year and a half in the warm climate of Southeast Asia before spending three years in San Diego. I was not looking forward to the cold, snowy New England weather. I had a friend drive me to Newport, and then I bought a ticket for him to fly back to Oklahoma. That way I could drink all the way there.

Alcoholism is a devastating and deadly disease. I believe that the alcoholic's soul is also sick from it. People around me could see my alcohol tainted behavior; but God could also see my sick soul. I later asked myself, "How could anyone see life with an intoxicated soul?"

One big problem with alcohol is how it distorts one's thoughts. It's a bad thing for an alcoholic to do a lot of thinking. I really lived my life between my own ears, with my distorted thoughts as a reference, which is a bad way to live.

Marian "Pat" Benedict Cmdr. USN NC Ret.

The Silence of the Pain is Deafening

I can look back to my childhood and see the personality traits of an alcoholic to be. I never felt like I fit in: there was everybody else, and then there was me. There was an emptiness, a loneliness in my core. I was always an outsider. I was always restless inside, searching for something elusive; some sort of stillness beyond me. In other words: instant alcoholic, just add some drinks.

In Newport I was drinking heavily, and drinking alone. Many times it was the corpsmen under me and not me who ran the operating room. Sometimes my hands were shaking too much to do the paperwork, so others would do it for me. At first, I had trouble getting along with the chief surgeon. After an early confrontation, though, we got along. When he left, he said I was the best OR nurse he had ever had.

Yet, as the Big Book of Alcohol Anonymous says, I was restless, angry and discontent. I began to realize that as one day departs, it goes into another drunken day. Meanwhile, the physical signs of my excessive drinking were obvious, but they were attributed to other causes. The Navy hospital at Newport was the second hospital where they thought that my shaking and vomiting were from gall bladder problems or some other cause, like the ulcers I was developing. I began to drink my alcohol with milk to tame my ulcers.

My Story

Alcoholism: My Prison Within My Soul

My drinking was mostly a way to protect myself from depression and emotional pain. There was the pain I carried with me from childhood, as well as the pain I endured during the fifteen months I spent aboard the Repose in Vietnam. Drinking as a defense against pain is a very lonely way to go. The one in pain really needs other people, but the drinker will push them away and retreat into his or her self. I stopped going to church and I stopped associating with the other nurses. I thought more alcohol was the way to find comfort; the way to still the storm within me.

During the three years I was stationed at Rhode Island, I never took any leave; I never went home. I didn't want to go home. I thought: "Why go argue with my mother?" Actually, I was hiding from myself how ashamed my mother was of my drinking; I was hiding so much of the outside world from myself that I seemed to have no feelings for anyone or anything. I began to think that my inner-self was faulty.

Then it began. I was hospitalized for the third time at Newport. I had complained of chest pains and vomiting, so they sent an ambulance. After a few days and lots of tests, a doctor came in and gently asked if maybe, just maybe, did I drink a bit too much?

I was outraged. I came up out of my bed and told him I wouldn't dignify that question with an answer. He apologized

Marian "Pat" Benedict Cmdr. USN NC Ret.

The Silence of the Pain is Deafening

and left the room. Then the chief of Cardiology came in and confronted me. He said my heart was fine, but that I had a drinking problem. That's when I gave in and admitted that maybe I did, on occasion, drink just a little too much. He didn't buy that. He told me that he had informed the chief of nursing.

When I was released from the hospital I was told to report to the chief of nursing. When I walked in she didn't even look up. She said, "The next time you pick up a drink, you are out of the Navy." She sent me to the Navy Psychiatrist.

I managed to go the entire weekend without a drink. Then Monday night I began to drink. I struggled for months to try to control my drinking. It turned out that the Psychiatrist graduated from the University of Oklahoma. We were fellow Oklahomans and things got a bit more relaxed. He finally told me to cut down on my drinking, and I said, "Sure, no problem." It was a problem.

Of course it was a problem, and somewhere inside I knew I had a problem. One time when the chief nurse was away, I talked to a doctor whom I knew went to AA meetings. I approached him when he was washing his hands, preparing for surgery. I asked very quietly if he went to AA meetings, but he responded in a normal tone: "Sure, would you like to go to an AA meeting with me?"

My Story

Alcoholism: My Prison Within My Soul

I said, "Not so loud!" Alcoholics typically believe that their drinking problem is unknown to others. It turned out that the doctor had known for months that I had a drinking problem but he knew better than to confront me and alienate me.

He came to pick me up for my first meeting. I had a couple of drinks just before he got there, and of course he could smell it on me, but he didn't say anything. We walked into the AA meeting in Newport and my first thought was: "I've gotta get out of here!" I stayed for the meeting, but I didn't like it. I didn't go back.

The next few months were a living hell. I never want to go through anything like that again. I was desperately trying to still the storm within me, while trying to control my alcoholism, as one drunken day departed and I crawled into the next. I developed a spiritual malignancy, and I didn't even care. I don't ever want to experience that again.

One drunken night I sat on the bed and loaded a small handgun, a revolver I owned, placing bullets one by one into the cylinder. I put the gun to my head and fired. I actually missed; the bullet went up by my head and put a hole in the ceiling. I then held the barrel squarely to my temple to make sure I wouldn't miss, and I tried again. The gun just clicked. I thought: "Whaaat??" I fell back on the bed, trying to concentrate, and I passed out drunk. The next morning I woke

Marian "Pat" Benedict Cmdr. USN NC Ret.

up with a bullet next to my head. I had dropped it when I was loading bullets into the chambers of the cylinder. If it had been in the gun I would not have woken; I would have been dead.

Then came the weekend that changed my life. I was on call for the Operating Room. I would never get drunk when I was on OR call. But that weekend I did, for reasons I can't explain. A corpsman called me and told me I was needed in the operating room. I was so drunk I have only bits and pieces of memories; I was blacking out. I don't remember driving there but I remember changing into my operating room greens. I remembered some parts of working but most of it was a blackout.

The next Monday a Psychiatrist came into the OR and told me to give the narcotics keys to another nurse and to go with him for a private talk. He took me into the nurse's restroom. He said I was going to be medevacked, airlifted, to Long Beach for treatment of alcoholism.

I outranked him, and so I looked him in the eye and demanded: "And if I don't want to go?!"

"Then you can face a court martial," he replied.

I said I'd go.

One of my corpsmen escorted me home, where I gathered a few things. I went to my bar and took up a bottle of vodka. The corpsman said, "Please don't."

Alcoholism: My Prison Within My Soul

I put the bottle back. He drove me back to the hospital, where I was admitted. There was a great amount of pain and misery within me as I faced detox, but there was also a feeling of relief in there amongst it all.

I was in a bed, shaking and sweating, beginning withdrawals, and none of the Navy nurses except the one on duty came in to see me. That evening one of my corpsmen came to take me to an AA meeting there on the hospital grounds. I hadn't known they had meetings there. Someone handed me a cup of coffee. I was shaking so badly I spilled it all over. I hardly slept that night, sweating and shaking and nauseated as I was.

The next morning, Captain Baker, the Commanding Officer of the Medical Corps came in to talk to me. I grabbed him by the shoulders and said, "You son of a bitch!"

He didn't seem to mind my manner. He told me that I was being medevacked out in an Air Force chopper.

So it must have been that my last drink was on December 22, 1972, although I don't remember it; I was blacked out at the time.

On Christmas Eve, 1972, I arrived at Long Beach, California. The Navy ambulance driver picked me up and I asked him if we could maybe stop for a quick drink. He looked at me as if he thought I should be locked up, and then he told

Marian "Pat" Benedict Cmdr. USN NC Ret.

The Silence of the Pain is Deafening

me sternly that he was to take me directly to the emergency room at the Naval Hospital. And that he did.

The next day the Navy Chaplain came in for a Christmas Day visit. I told him to get the hell out and he backed out. It was many weeks later that I finally went to him to apologize. While I was at the hospital they found out that I had some cracked ribs. Something I gained, no doubt from one or more falls. I also had a swollen liver, which I'm sure wasn't a surprise.

A few days after Christmas, Commander Dick Jewell came by to drive me from the hospital down to the Navy Base in Long Beach, where I began my long road to recovery.

Chapter Nine
Treatment: The Click that Unlocked the Lock

The Silence of the Pain is Deafening

I desperately needed a catalyst (sobriety)
to awaken my consciousness.
In the next three months of treatment
I slowly realized that getting sober
was like taking the bars off of the windows.

Dick Jewell picked me up at the Naval Hospital in Long Beach, CA, and then drove me down to the Naval Station. The way he drove, I wondered if we would make it alive. On the way down Dick told me that Captain Joe Zuska, USN Medical Corps, was head of the naval alcohol program.

I thought to myself: "Who cares! I don't belong there!"

> **The Birth of the Navy Alcohol Treatment Centers**
>
> In 1965, a newly recovering alcoholic and retired Navy Commander, Dick Jewell turned the alcoholism problem in the US Navy on its ear.
> Dr. Joseph J. Zuska was then the Senior Medical Officer at the Long Beach, Calif. Naval Station on Terminal Island. Dick Jewell walked into Dr. Zuska's office and asked the Captain why the Navy wasn't doing more about alcoholism. Dr. Zuska had no answer for him, and

I had my game plan worked out: I would tell this captain that he was a surgeon, and thus wouldn't know about alcoholism, and that I was a Registered Nurse and so I was trained in the area of alcohol abuse, the symptoms of which I did not have. I simply didn't belong here, and that was that.

My Story

Treatment: The Click that Unlocked the Lock

As we walked into Captain Zuska's office I saluted him and then I said, "I don't belong here; there is some mistake."

He stood up –the man was well over six feet tall- and told me: "Sit down and be quiet."

He was quite an imposing man, so I did as he said.

Well, I didn't get a chance to argue my side of it because we didn't talk much about my "so called" drinking problem; I rather learned about the living arrangements. It seemed I would be about the only female around. Also, less attention would be paid to rank.

As the only female patient, I was to live in the BOQ –the Bachelor Officer Quarters. All of the counselors were male officers or enlisted men. My counselor was to be a Chief Petty Officer. The officers and enlisted men would be in the same group for counseling and they would all eat chow together. However, when the patients were taken to

Dick Jewell

Marian "Pat" Benedict Cmdr. USN NC Ret.

The Silence of the Pain is Deafening

the AA meeting, the officers would ride in separate vans from the enlisted men.

My memories of the first few days in treatment are a little blurred. There was one female Psychologist, a civilian. We had a Navy Psychiatrist, Bill Rader, and a Navy Doctor who gave me my physical. I had a large bruise on my left arm, which I couldn't explain. Also, I had told the doctor that I had trouble breathing deeply and he found two cracked ribs. A couple of days later I recovered a partial memory of having fallen down my basement stairs back in Newport. Otherwise I was in pretty good shape, except for my swollen liver.

On the surface during those early days I alternated between depression, anger and loneliness, while really, down inside, I was plagued with denial and fear.

The program mostly consisted of group therapy each morning after roll call, and an AA meeting each night, somewhere out in the local community.

> so they decided it was time for a change.
> The first AA meeting (they named it Dry Dock) was held in a WWII Quonset hut. As sailors and others became sober, some of them stayed on as counselors. There soon came to be a mix of naval officers and enlisted men, Marines and Coast Guard members among the counselors.
> At first officers and enlisted men were grouped separately, but eventually that was aborted and all

My Story

Treatment: The Click that Unlocked the Lock

My second day in treatment was my first time in group therapy. I walked into the room with about five other patients. The counselor was an enlisted man, Len Baitzer, whom I had already made up my mind to dislike. After we read from the 24 hour book, Len looked at me and asked, "Where is your uniform?"

I replied, "Ask God."

Len didn't flinch; he went right on with the group therapy session. At some later time my uniform finally arrived from the east coast. The staff seemed pleased by the arrival, but I really didn't care.

As time went on my head began to clear up. At least my thinking process improved, but not so much my attitude. This was supposed to be a four week program, so after four weeks I expected to hear about how soon I would be discharged. Not hearing anything, I asked to see the Big Man; the Head Honcho; "King Whatever."

> of the patients were treated together (the concept of hierarchy runs counter to the AA philosophy). Eventually the alcoholism program piloted by the Navy was copied by the other branches of the Service.
>
> Now, many decades later, thousands of military men and women owe much gratitude- in some cases they owe their lives- to Dr. Joseph J. Zuska and Dick Jewell, Captain, USN Ret.

Marian "Pat" Benedict Cmdr. USN NC Ret.

The Silence of the Pain is Deafening

He was sitting at his desk, reaching for his phone when I walked in. I saluted and declared: "I want out of here!"

He replied, "Go back to your group. I'll talk to you later." Then he went about his business without another glance at me.

I stepped back, saluted again and then kicked his desk good and hard. He didn't even look up, which was good, since I could barely walk out without limping. It felt like I had broken some bones in my foot, but it turned out I hadn't.

A lot of my fellow patients were being discharged from the treatment program. They would then return to their duty stations. And then there was me. Some six or seven weeks after I began the program, I was just beginning to understand that I was not a well person. Throughout my treatment, my life was ruled by fear. Every alcoholic I have met is ruled, at least to some extent, by fear. But there was I, the Vietnam vet, the Nave Nurse Corps Commander, with my life ruled entirely by fear. I felt as if I were caught in a box with no way out.

As my treatment progressed, I began to look back on myself; I thought that my heart was faulty. As a drinker I thought that "last" was a good place to be: last to forgive someone; last to help; last to care. I learned that half of the alcoholic is never seen or known by others; half of who we are is hidden, buried.

My Story

Treatment: The Click that Unlocked the Lock

Not long after my treatment began, I met Martha. We were dynamically different: I came from poverty; she from wealth. But we hit it off. The following year I returned to the Navy alcohol treatment program to work, and Martha became my sponsor (effectively: a *mentor* –Ed).

In treatment it seemed as if only surface issues were dealt with. For example, my experience in Vietnam was scarcely touched upon. That was a mistake, since I had to deal with Vietnam in depth in order to stay sober. Most of us in treatment didn't think we had such a problem with alcohol that we needed to be forcibly detoxed and treated; in fact, at first, most of us wouldn't admit we had any problem at all. My own treatment, and my observations of others in the group became important learning experiences for me, as I was destined to join the other side, so I could help others.

During the early stages of treatment I didn't sleep well. My thoughts would alternate as I lay awake at night. Would I stay sober and stay in the Navy, or would I just drop out and drink? Or maybe: drink, get kicked out, and then drink some more. I would contemplate a life of petty crime to support my drinking. There was a constant urge to drink, and I could justify almost anything which would result from drinking, or which could accommodate it. I would think, "No, my life is the Navy." Then I would think, "But I want a drink."

Marian "Pat" Benedict Cmdr. USN NC Ret.

The Silence of the Pain is Deafening

Sometimes in group I would look at myself and think, "I should grow up and stop being such an ass." Then I would think: "We should all go out and have a drink." Day in, day out, every thought seemed to lead to: "It's time for a drink."

I had hidden from myself how ashamed my mother was of my alcoholism. Captain Zuska told me that he had received a letter from my mother, expressing her shame at my drinking. I almost vomited. For a moment I wished that I hadn't failed when I tried to shoot myself, years before. I shut down and dropped into depression. It took weeks to get over it. My mother had more power over me than I was able to admit or to cope with. I didn't come to terms with that until after she died.

One time, after a couple of months in treatment, I walked into group therapy and the counselor Len told me that I would be spending some time with another counselor, one named Archie Tyler (a short, African American enlisted man).

I said, "The hell I am!"

Len replied, "You're going; just go." Len told me to go back to my room and to change out of my uniform and into some slacks, and then wait for Archie to come pick me up. I couldn't figure out why I should wear slacks.

When Archie came by, climbing in the car I asked him, "Where are we going?"

Archie answered, "The bowling alley."

Treatment: The Click that Unlocked the Lock

I about fell out of the car. I said, "The hell we are!" But Archie just smiled. He smiled a lot.

I thought: "He's crazy or I'm crazy!"

But after about a half hour of bowling, I began to smile, too. Then I began to laugh. Archie wasn't trying to make me laugh, he was just a naturally funny guy. As he is today, about four decades later. I know because we play a little golf now and again. I love him dearly and I still confide in him.

In that bowling alley, I was surprised at myself for laughing. I couldn't remember the last time I had laughed. But laughing was a breakthrough for me, as if a door began to open and a part of me was looking out from inside the storm shelter.

A few days later, I was awake in the middle of the night, thinking about all that had happened. I began to think that maybe I did have a drinking problem. I thought that maybe I was an alcoholic; that the roots of my alcoholism took hold with my first drink. I was always an outsider; I never fit in; I felt a terrible loneliness within, since I could not get close to anyone. I felt those things since my childhood. Then I discovered that I could change everything with a drink. And so it began. I felt closer to my sister when we began to drink together. That was important to me, but really: I felt like I could fit in anywhere when I drank.

Marian "Pat" Benedict Cmdr. USN NC Ret.

The Silence of the Pain is Deafening

One of the most difficult parts of treatment was expressing my feelings during group therapy. Opening up to the others in the group is a very important aspect of therapy. Without it there's no benefit from being in a group. But I wasn't brought up that way. We never expressed our feelings in my family. The concept was alien to me, and there I was, expected to open up to a group of people I didn't know very well. I was afraid that if I began to express my inner feelings, the others there would know me, and at that point I didn't really know me. I would have been learning what Pat was all about right along with the rest of them. Exposing myself was an irrevocable act that scared me.

One of the routines in AA is the hug. Everyone hugs everyone. This, too was alien to me, since my family wasn't the huggy type. I really didn't know how to go around the room hugging people. It took me months to figure out how group therapy worked and how AA worked. It took me months to learn the way that mutual love and respect, and mutual acceptance, in a room full of equals, can break down the walls, expose the inner self and facilitate repairs within. With the inner self exposed, denial, the alcoholic's worst enemy, becomes obvious when it raises its head. This was all very new to me. Mutual love and respect, openness and social egalitarianism weren't to be found in the household where I

Treatment: The Click that Unlocked the Lock

grew up (those principals aren't part of the military social order, either).

It was during my third and last month of treatment that I really began to heal. My fear subsided and my anger began to lift; I began to listen and understand. At the end of March of 1973, I was told that I would soon be discharged and that I would return to my duty station in Newport, Rhode Island. My response to Captain Zuska was to say, "No, no, no! Not Newport!" I was certain the chief nurse there hated me.

His reply was: "You are going."

Of course I wanted to leave treatment, but I also wanted to stay. The program was beginning to grow on me. Rehab programs can be very supportive, once one stops fighting them. A few years later Captain Zuska explained to me that he had sent me back, over my objections, because he wanted me to break free from rehab and to enter the world again.

I stopped by Oklahoma City on the way back, to make amends with my mother. I don't recall that she said anything; I think she was unresponsive. When I arrived at Newport, the Chief Nurse was on leave. She soon returned, however, and she and I had a long talk. We ended up very good friends. I also made amends with Captain Baker, the Commanding Officer who originally ordered me into rehab. Today we are

Marian "Pat" Benedict Cmdr. USN NC Ret.

still close friends; I call him every December 22nd (my AA birthday) and thank him for my life.

Captain Baker and I

I was no longer working in the OR at the Newport Naval Hospital; upon my return I was put in Obstetrics, in the Delivery Room. It was only a mild disappointment, since I liked Obstetrics; I just would have preferred the OR. For most of the rest of 1973, I spent my spare time at Dr. Joe O'Donnell and his wife Sandy's house. I ate a lot of meals there and Dr. Joe and I went to a lot of AA meetings together- God bless them both!

By December of 1973, I was helping Dr. Joe with the AA meetings in various ways. I really liked Alcoholics Anonymous. At the hospital, some of the Navy staff nurses began to confide in me concerning their own drinking problems and about the drinking problems in their own families.

Treatment: The Click that Unlocked the Lock

In December of 1973 I received orders to return to the Naval Hospital in Long Beach, California to work in the Alcohol Rehab Department. They said they needed a recovering alcoholic female to be the Department Nurse. I drove sober back to Oklahoma City, and my mother drove with me to Long Beach.

Marian "Pat" Benedict Cmdr. USN NC Ret.

Chapter Nine

Friends are a Gift of Sobriety

Future Assumptions

One of the things I was taught through Alcoholics Anonymous was to take life 'One Day at a Time.' So I try to live neither in the past, nor in assumptions about what the future might bring. When I was in detox in 1972, I could not have imagined that six years later I would be bringing a former First Lady to that same place for treatment of chemical dependency and alcoholism. Back then, I wanted to give up, walk out and have a drink as it was; maybe if I knew what the future held, I would have.

In April of 1978 I was still on active duty in the Navy, and since 1973, I had been assigned to the Navy Alcohol Rehabilitation Center at the Naval Hospital in Long Beach, California. The center needed a Navy nurse and a recovering alcoholic and that was me. I still had another year to go on chemotherapy for breast cancer. I had had a radical mastectomy, the complete removal of my right breast, but I was doing pretty well.

The Navy Alcoholics Anonymous group was called the Dry Dock and it met once a week on Thursday evenings from 8:00 to 9:30 pm. I was the Treasurer, and I always attended the meeting. One Thursday evening, after the meeting had been going on a while, our Navy counselor on duty motioned to me. I approached and he indicated the phone. I picked up the phone

Friends are a Gift of Sobriety

and found that my boss, Captain Pursch, was on the other end. He asked if I was at the meeting alone and I said yes (thinking to myself that it was none of his business if I was alone or not). He told me to stay and finish the meeting and then to come to his house alone. I thought to myself that he would ask me to pick up someone at one of the airports.

We preferred to pick up our prospective clients from the airport, since they might be in no condition to drive. A corpsman would be an adequate chauffer for most clients, but for someone of notoriety or rank, I was sometimes chosen. We had treated President Carter's brother, Billy, for example. Billy Carter turned out to be a real nice guy. We also treated Senator Herman Talmadge and astronaut Buz Aldrin, among others. So I drove to Captain Joseph Pursch's house, thinking I knew the future, that I would be going to the airport. How wrong I was.

Captain Joseph Pursch, a flight surgeon and a psychiatrist, was Director of the Alcohol Rehabilitation Service at the Naval Regional Medical Center in Long Beach, California. He was born in Chicago and raised in Yugoslavia. When he returned to the US, he graduated from Indiana University School of Medicine and specialized in Psychiatry. As a Navy Flight Surgeon he served aboard the aircraft carrier USS Forrestal. He holds the Distinguished Service Medal from the

Marian "Pat" Benedict Cmdr. USN NC Ret.

President of United States. He has served on both President Carter's Commission on Alcoholism and President Reagan's Blue Ribbon Commission on Drunk Driving.

I've Volunteered You

I arrived at Captain Pursch's house and his wife Irene showed me to the living room, saying that the Captain would be down in a few minutes. He came bouncing down the stairs and asked, "What do you know about Betty Ford?"

I looked at him and said, "I don't know any Betty Ford. Is she a Navy nurse?"

He prompted: "I was talking about the former First Lady, Betty Ford."

I almost laughed, but he seemed serious. I asked, "How in the hell would I know about her?"

He explained that Betty Ford's daughter Susan had talked to a Gynecologist, a Dr. Joe Cruse, who was also a recovering alcoholic. Susan confided that her mother was on prescription medication and was ill. Captain Pursch went on to say that Dr. Cruise had called him, and it was eventually decided by President Ford and the former First Family to do an intervention.

I thought to myself, "Well, that sounds like a good idea and I hope it goes well." But I also wondered why he was telling me all of this.

Friends are a Gift of Sobriety

Captain Pursch may have read my mind. He announced: "You are going down to Rancho Mirage tomorrow morning and help on this intervention. If all goes well you will stay at the house about a week and, –again, if all goes well– later she will be admitted to the Long Beach Navy Rehabilitation Center."

I learned later that Captain Pursch had told Dr. Cruse that he was bringing his nurse (me).

Dr. Cruse had responded: "I don't know her."

Captain Pursch proceeded to tell him that I was a full Commander, a female, a recovering alcoholic, and that I had had a radical mastectomy (when she was First Lady, Betty had gained admiration and gratitude when she made her mastectomy public, reducing the stigma). Captain Pursch told me later that I was just the right person at the right time and that Betty  and I had a lot in common. As it turned out, he was right: Betty and I eventually were a match (though I don't recall my ever being a First Lady).

Marian "Pat" Benedict Cmdr. USN NC Ret.

The Silence of the Pain is Deafening

"Wait a minute," I said. "If you just walk off with me I think the Commanding Officer and Chief Nurse would wonder where the hell I was."

All that, he said, was taken care of and if anyone asked where I was, including our staff, they would be told that my mother was ill and I was on emergency leave. Later I found out that some of the staff sent her get well cards and she didn't know why or where on earth I was.

I had been sitting in an AA meeting minding my own business, and the next thing I knew I was about to be involved in intervention in the life of a former First Lady I had never met. I learned not plan my life too far ahead. I was to be at Captain Pursch's house at 0700 the next morning in civilian clothes. He made it clear: no Navy uniform.

Many times I have thought back on that evening and I'm certain he never asked, "Do you want to do this?"

I arrived at his door at 0700 in civilian clothes with a small suitcase. This was on Friday, March 31, 1978. The intervention was to take place the next day. I don't recall being nervous or scared; I was kind of on auto-pilot, as all of this hadn't yet been processed in my mind. Military training does that to you: you follow orders now and think about it later. Captain Pursch and I had dinner with Dr. Cruse at his house in Rancho Mirage, and then I spent the night there.

My Story

Friends are a Gift of Sobriety

Susan: Originator, Organizer

Susan had rounded up her father, President Ford, who was on a speaking engagement. He flew home. She had already called her brother Michael, who came from the East Coast, and her other two brothers, Jack and Steve, who lived nearby. Susan also arranged for Claire, their old housekeeper back before Gerald Ford became President, to fly in. Susan wanted her there: since she knew the old secrets of home life with Betty, her very presence would be accusatory. Poor Betty had no idea that any of this was taking place.

We, that is: President Ford, Michael and his wife Gayle, Susan, Jack, Steve, Claire, Dr. Cruse, Captain Pursch and I, met in President Ford's at-home office, which was in a building separate from the main house. After everyone understood their role and what to say in an intervention, we went over to the house.

Intervention

Needless to say, when her entire family walked in, Betty was surprised. Then, behind the family came Claire and Dr. Cruse, and finally, Capt. Pursch and me. Betty had no idea who we were and she seemed less than pleased.

I remember President Ford being the first one to speak, and then the rest of the family took turns after him. Then Claire also added some details. It was much later that Betty told me that the one family member who really got to her in the intervention was Gayle, who is Mike's wife. Gayle said something which really hit home for Betty. These interventions can get deep and personal.

Susan, the 19 year old daughter who started all of this, sat on my left, holding my hand, squeezing it tightly. Interventions are done with love, as they can be difficult for everyone. When all had said what they wanted to say, President Ford told Betty that I would be staying for a few days at the house. She wasn't pleased about that, I had guessed, but she didn't show it outwardly. I told her that I also had had a mastectomy and in fact I was still on chemotherapy. She gave a little smile and lightly patted my cheek. I don't think she liked me very much, but thankfully, that changed over time.

Detox

My boss, Captain Pursch, sent Dr. Cruse and me to the nearby Eisenhower Medical Center for the medication to detoxify Betty at home. Captain Pursch didn't wish me good luck or even say goodbye. He just left. As I've said to Captain Pursch since, we were either very brilliant, or very lucky. She could have died. As it was, she suffered some significant withdrawal symptoms, even with the medication. Betty leaned on me as she suffered, and then we began to become friends as she recovered from the withdrawals.

My Story

Friends are a Gift of Sobriety

Family Warmth

The Ford's house wasn't fancy; it was just a basic three-bedroom unit. The thing that struck me was how down to earth the family was. In fact, the day after the intervention I saw President Ford in the kitchen in his bathrobe putting dirty dishes into the dishwasher. Jack and Steve had put a rollaway bed for me in the study close the Fords' bedroom.

A few days after the intervention, when Betty was feeling better, I took her outside for a little walk. She wore a simple blue and white skirt with a white top. Before we started out I turned to her and said, "I will walk with you forever; however, it is impossible for me to walk *for* you."

She turned and looked at me and said simply, "Well, if we are going to walk, let's walk." She put her arm around my shoulders, and off we went.

A day later President Ford woke me at about 5 am. He said he was going out of town but would be back late that evening. He related to me as if I were a family member. I lay back down and looked at the ceiling. I thought, "How did I get into this? I'm not even a Republican!"

A little later I went to the bedroom to check on Betty. She told me to get in President Ford's side of the bed and in about an hour we could get up and go into the den and have our coffee and read the papers. Betty's intervention and detox was

Marian "Pat" Benedict Cmdr. USN NC Ret.

much like any other, as the Fords were much like any other family (although perhaps a little warmer than most).

They had a large swimming pool, which President Ford swam in almost daily. One day Betty said to me, "Why don't you go and have a swim?"

I said that I didn't have a bathing suit, and she said, "Just go in in your birthday suit –no one can see you."

There was a high wall around the pool so… that is what I did.

Rehab Center

The intervention was on a Saturday, April 1, and towards the end of the week we informed Betty that she was going to be an inpatient at a treatment center, beginning the next week. The Fords were all very supportive of Betty. They celebrated her birthday with her on Sunday and she first went to the treatment center in Long Beach on Monday, April 10th, 1978, where Betty was brought into a four-bed room and shown her bed.

She looked around and said, "I am not staying."

I thought: "All that work for nothing!" I went straight down to Captain Pursch, to see what could be done for her.

Captain Pursch came up to the room and told Betty that he would ask the other ladies to move. He said something to the effect of: 'You want a private room, here's your private room.'

Friends are a Gift of Sobriety

Well, as it turned out, no one had to move. Betty was officially checked in the following morning, and she stayed in the four-bed room with the other women. There weren't any private rooms at this Navy facility; officers and enlisted men were randomly bunked together. Rehab programs are designed around the idea that people are best able to help and support their peers when they are in the same (difficult) situation. Such concepts as hierarchy and rank are thus counter-productive.

Betty did very well there. Everyone on the staff and the other inpatients welcomed her and no fuss or special attention was given her. When she had the Betty Ford Center built at Rancho Mirage, she made sure that there were no private rooms.

A Covert Mission

During the 10 days that I was gone, everyone at work thought that I was in Oklahoma, taking care of my mother. I found out later that Captain Pursch's secretary, Betty Disney, had called my mother at home. She had previously met my mother and called to ask how she was.

My mom told her, "I'm fine."

Then Ms. Disney asked her if I was there and my mother said no. After a little more conversation they hung up, each a bit perplexed. My mother called my sister, worried that I had gone back to drinking.

Marian "Pat" Benedict Cmdr. USN NC Ret.

The Silence of the Pain is Deafening

My sister told her, "Mom, don't worry so much. She is probably doing something for Dr. Pursch."

Of course after I had gotten Betty Ford to Long Beach I called my mother and told her where I had been for the last 10 days.

A few years later when my mom and I were invited to the President and Mrs. Ford's home, President Ford hugged my mother, kissed her on the cheek and said, "Thank you for your daughter."

Mom said to him, "Oh, that's okay, I just didn't know where she was for 10 days," and we all laughed.

Family Friend

While Betty was in treatment I went with her to her evening AA meetings. We never announced which meeting she would be going to because the crowds would show up. Of course we had to have Secret Service agents with us. We usually went in the back door of the meetings. I used to tease her that before I started hanging out with her I was allowed in the front door. After a few weeks in the treatment center, Betty was discharged.

Betty did so well after her treatment that I thought that I would rarely hear from her, my services not being required. I thought that at most we would exchange Christmas cards and the like.

Friends are a Gift of Sobriety

How wrong I was. We talked and visited often, even before she built the Betty Ford Center. We became close friends. I spent a few Thanksgivings with her and the family, and I also went down to the desert (Rancho Mirage) often on weekends and was even invited several times to their home in Beaver Creek, Colorado. I asked nothing of her or her family; the friendship itself was so greatly valued. A gift indeed, of sobriety!

The Beaver Creek house was warm and comfortable – nothing fancy. President Ford loved to ski, so they bought the house for ski-getaways, but then kept it after he quit skiing.

One time when I was at Beaver Creek, their son Steve was also there. Betty told President Ford and Steve that we were going to an AA meeting and would be back in a couple of hours.

Steve jokingly asked his dad, "How do you know they're really going to a meeting?"

President Ford replied, "When those two get together who knows where they go or what they do."

Marian "Pat" Benedict Cmdr. USN NC Ret.

The Silence of the Pain is Deafening

On another trip to Beaver Creek, Betty and I decided to play a joke on two assistants. I was surprised when President Ford agreed to play along. Neither President Ford's assistant, Penny, nor Betty's secretary, Ann Cullen, were married. Since I too was single we would talk about our having that in common. The two assistants would gripe about not having fiancés, or even boyfriends. On this par-  ticular trip I showed up with a ring –costume jewelry, really– on my left hand ring finger. Betty was upstairs, combing her hair, when I came in and showed her the ring. We agreed to play a joke on the girls.

I went down to the office and, in a casual way, made sure they could see the ring. Needless to say they both got excited. I told them I had accepted the ring from my boyfriend and was contemplating getting married. After we talked they flew upstairs to confirm this fact of an impending marriage. Betty said she had to keep from laughing. She lowered her head so

Friends are a Gift of Sobriety

they wouldn't see her face. She said that if Pat said she was seriously thinking of marriage it must be true. She made some

remark to the effect that "you girls better get busy and find some boyfriends."

A little while later President Ford came through the room to say goodbye, since he was going on a short trip. We heard later that he told Ann and Penny, "As I guess the both of you heard, Pat is seriously thinking of getting married. She asked me if I would give her away and I told her it would be my pleasure." And out the door he went.

We ran with that joke for several months. The Fords had such fun with it, until the three of us, President Ford, Betty and I, confessed. Even decades later President Ford would bring the subject up, and I still cannot get over how cool and convincing he was that day.

Marian "Pat" Benedict Cmdr. USN NC Ret.

Military Retirement

Late in 1979, as my retirement date approached, I was teaching a course on substance abuse at the El Toro Marine base, as I had every month for about two years. I was lecturing a typical class of 30 to 35 Marines, when we heard: "Attention on Deck!"

It actually shook me up. I gathered my wits as everyone else jumped to attention, and then I did also. It was the Commanding General of the base. He walked up to me; I saluted him and he saluted me. Then told the troops to be seated.

He said, "I hear you are going to retire next month."

I replied: "Yes sir."

He said that he would like for the Marine Corps at El Toro to do the honors. Well, my Marine students all stood up and applauded. I was honored, not to mention touched, and I told him I would be honored, that is: if my Commanding Officer at the Naval Hospital would allow that. He told me he had already asked the CO at the Hospital and the Chief Nurse and they were very pleased. So it was all systems go. The Naval Medical Corps cares for Marines in addition to naval personnel; even so, there had only been one other Navy nurse ever to be retired by the Marines.

Friends are a Gift of Sobriety

A Letter from the President

When I told Betty about it, she wanted to come. President Ford was going to be out of town, but he wrote me a letter

GERALD R. FORD

Nov. 27, 1979

Dear Pat:

Our whole family is deeply indebted to you and we thank you for your many kindnesses. More importantly we are grateful for your friendship.

You have done a superb job in the U.S. Navy — "well done" from a former Commander in Chief.

You have our love and warmest best wishes.

Jerry Ford

which is transcribed below:

Marian "Pat" Benedict Cmdr. USN NC Ret.

The Silence of the Pain is Deafening

Dear Pat,

Our whole family is deeply indebted to you and we thank you for your many kindnesses. More importantly we are grateful for your friendship.

You have done a superb job in the U.S. Navy– "well done," from a former Commander in Chief.

You have our love and warmest best wishes.

Jerry Ford

The General's wife prepared a nice lunch for me, which was served before the ceremony. Betty Ford sat with us, and my mother did as well. Two of my cousins, Margot Yeck and Rick Carroll, came from Oklahoma and shared in the lunch. Captain Pursch attended, as did his secretary, Betty Disney,

Friends are a Gift of Sobriety

along with her son Jeff. Captain Pursch's wife, Irene also ate with us.

The ceremony was held outside on the Parade Grounds. My special guests sat together on chairs set up for them. My mom sat by Betty Ford and the General's wife. A Navy Photographer was on hand and several Navy nurses from the Naval Hospital were there. A marine held the leash of the Marine Bull Dog mascot who was wearing the marine coat.

After the ceremony my Navy nurse friends asked me: "How did you pull this off: being retired by the Marines?!"

I just smiled in reply.

After a Marine Officer spoke, Captain Pursch spoke and presented me with the Navy Commendation Medal and I also

Marian "Pat" Benedict Cmdr. USN NC Ret.

got to inspect the Marine Troops. I think some of those guys fought back a smile, seeing a woman doing the Inspection.

From the left: Irene Pursch, Cpt. Pursch, my mom, Betty Ford, Commanding General's wife

While my mother and Betty sat together, watching the ceremony, my mother said to her: "Pat will be all right. She is close to tears, but she will be okay." To be honest, I had to swallow those tears, I was so moved by it all.

Thanksgiving Prayer

On one of the times that I was invited to spend Thanksgiving with the Fords, I was struck with what a typical family they were. President Ford was at the head of the table;

Friends are a Gift of Sobriety

I was to his right, with Steve next to me. Betty was at the other end of the table and Jack sat across from Steve and me.

We all held hands as President Ford began the prayer. After a little while Steve whispered, "Dad, you're not giving a speech."

It took all I had to keep from bursting out laughing. Steve looked at me and smiled, while President Ford just kept on with his prayer.

The Center

a hug from Steve

About four or five years after the intervention Betty called me and wanted to know if I could come down for the weekend. President Ford was going to be away and she wanted company. I really didn't think too much about it, since I had been down there many times, both when President Ford was there, and when he was not. As I walked in the door Betty hugged me and kissed me on the cheek. I went and put my overnight bag in Susan's bedroom, which is where I stayed when I visited.

Marian "Pat" Benedict Cmdr. USN NC Ret.

The Silence of the Pain is Deafening

I walked into her little office and she looked up at me, smiling, and said, matter-of-factly: "I am going to build a treatment center for substance abuse and alcoholism."

I was in shock. I think I laughed, or started to. I finally found words: "You must be kidding?"

But she said she'd given it a lot of thought and prayer over the last few years and I realized she was sincere. It was to be built on the grounds of the Eisenhower Hospital which was near their home. In fact, you can walk to the hospital from their house. She had it all planned out and she was going to raise the money with others' help. She had never mentioned, at least to me, that she wanted to get involved in treating alcohol and drug abuse. She had been off of alcohol and prescription drugs for four, maybe five years. She had been clean, in fact, since the intervention itself (apart from the detox medication right at first). Our friendship quickly transcended matters of drug or alcohol dependency, so the subject rarely came up between us.

I said, half joking: "The good Lord works in strange ways."

She laughed, and then said: "And there will be no private rooms!"

We did lot of talking that weekend and she said, "You will always have a job at the Betty Ford Center."

I said, "Oh no, not a counselor: I have four different education jobs just now!" (I had started out teaching a non-credit course for nurses on Alcoholism and Chemical Dependency at Golden West Junior College, which then turned into a full three credit course, and then California State University at Long Beach hired me as an Associate Professor for their Master's program in Social Work. Additionally, I was a lecturer at Delinquency Control Institute at USC, and at the Police Administration Institute School of Public Administration, also there at the University of Southern California.)

But I thanked her for the offer. And that was the beginning of The Betty Ford Center. I was proud of her, as was President Ford, and he gave his full support, as did her children.

I said, "Betty, your legacy will be to open the door for women with substance abuse problems, and to remove once and for all the stigma."

Birthday Cake

As I mentioned before, we in Alcoholics Anonymous speak of the first day of sobriety as our birthday, in part to emphasize that life begins anew when drinking stops. Well, we actually do birthday cakes to mark the years. Since the addiction never ceases, sobriety is a continued effort, and so these birthday cakes serve as important reminders, lest we become complacent.

Well, I asked Betty if she would please do my 12th year cake in 1984. This was a lot to ask of her: not just that she had to travel to Huntington Beach, but of course, the Secret Service brought her, and since word leaked out, there was quite the crowd at the AA meeting. She wanted to say something to the crowd when she presented the cake to me, but since I hadn't asked her to, she wasn't sure. Several years later she asked me why I didn't ask her to speak. I didn't have a good answer for her. It is really a bit awkward sometimes: having such a famous friend. I think she understood.

Life Comes to a Close

President Ford was around 93 when he passed on in 2006. Betty was some five years younger. There was a local church gathering in which people would come to see Betty and to offer condolences. When I arrived, there was a long line of people waiting to say a few words to Betty.

Betty's son Steve spotted me, came over, hugged me and kissed me on the cheek. Steve put his arm around me and walked me to the front of the line and said, "Mom, look who's here."

Betty hugged me super tight and said, "Oh, Pat I am so glad you are here!"

I was personally invited to the service in Washington, DC but I declined, though it was an honor to have been invited. I knew there would be a lot of dignitaries there and I had already been to the viewing at Rancho Mirage. I had walked up to his

Friends are a Gift of Sobriety

American Flag-draped casket and I said what I wanted to say; I saluted his casket, and then I felt complete regarding his death, and I did not feel the need to go to the official ceremony in Washington.

Betty's health began to decline after President Ford passed on. During the last two years of her life, I went down often but I only visited for an hour or so each time. The last time I saw her was about a month or two before she died. She was very frail, but she was also alert and she could still be very funny.

On one visit, when I walked in the bedroom and kissed her on the cheek, she said, "Remember sitting on the floor beside this bed the night after the intervention?"

I related to her what I remembered: she was going through withdrawals from her prescription drugs, and when President Ford came in I asked him to go get a bowl or anything he could find so I could catch everything she threw up. She told me that that was the worst night she had ever had. And then she asked me which bowl he'd brought back (!). I do that myself sometimes: when I am recollecting some important event, I try to remember all the little details.

She scooted over in bed and said, "Sit here beside me and we can talk for a few minutes." She took my hand and said, "Do you remember what you said to me the first time you and I walked outside about 35 years ago?"

Marian "Pat" Benedict Cmdr. USN NC Ret.

The Silence of the Pain is Deafening

I affirmed, saying: "You had on a white top and a blue and white skirt."

Then I turned to her and repeated: "I will walk with you forever; however, it is impossible for me to walk *for* you."

I said to Betty, "You put your arm around my shoulder, looked up and said, 'Well, if we are going to walk, let's walk.' And so we did for 35 years."

Betty said to me, "I never forgot that."

That was the last time I ever saw or talked to her. Susan had Ann Cullen, Betty's secretary come family assistant, call me the day Betty died and tell me where the service would be held. I was seated behind the family, which I thought was very nice of them. Before the service a gentleman came and got me. He took me upstairs to the room where Betty's casket was and said, "The family thought you might like to spend a few minutes alone before they bring the casket into the church."

I said what I wanted to say to her, kissed her casket and said, "Betty, you done good!"

I also said a few words at her funeral. I read the Serenity Prayer, which Betty had chosen for me to read. Susan told me I would follow the grandkids. The three people who gave the tributes were chosen by Betty: Rosalynn Carter, Cokie Roberts and Geoffrey Mason. Though Jimmy Carter defeated President Ford in an election, Betty and Rosalynn were good

Friends are a Gift of Sobriety

friends. Rosalynn Carter had been doing a lot of work for the mentally ill. Cokie Roberts' father was in Congress the same time as President Ford. He was a Democrat and Gerald Ford a Republican, but they would eat together, arguing politics, and remain the best of friends. Geoffrey Mason was a former director of the Betty Ford Clinic.

A CELEBRATION OF THE LIFE OF
Elizabeth Bloomer Ford

April 8, 1918 — July 8, 2011

Marian "Pat" Benedict Cmdr. USN NC Ret.

The Silence of the Pain is Deafening

I was invited to go to Michigan, to the Ford presidential library, where Betty was to be buried next to President Ford, but I declined. I felt there was no unfinished business between us.

The family had a few guests at the house after the funeral. I was standing next to her son Mike and we both looked over to the couch where Betty had been sitting next to President Ford the day of the intervention.

Mike turned to me with a little smile on his face and said, "I don't think Mom liked you the first days of the intervention."

I told him I was not there for her to like me. I said that I was there to help her, to love her, to take care of her and to walk with her.

I stayed at the house after the funeral, to have some time with the family.

Susan gave me a hug and said, "Mom really loved you."

I got my usual hug and kiss from Steve– he is such a great guy. I love him, as I do Mike, Susan and Jack. I got to say hi to some of the grand kids. They are adults, some married with their own children. Gayle, Mike's wife was there. She was also involved in the intervention.

I said, "Gayle, I still remember what you said at the intervention."

Friends are a Gift of Sobriety

She replied, "Pat, I meant what I said."

Gayle is a great gal. I don't share what is said at interventions; those matters should remain private.

I would like to give a big thank you to my good friend Rod Clausen who drove me down to see Betty on many occasions and for her funeral. I love you!

Marian "Pat" Benedict Cmdr. USN NC Ret.

Chapter Ten
Death Row

The Silence of the Pain is Deafening

*I*f someone had asked me if I thought that one day I might be in the Death Row section of the penitentiary in McAlester, Oklahoma, I would have suspected some mental instability. So, should I now suspect myself of having a screw or two loose? The answer is: we never know where God may lead us. Now that I have talked to, and made a study of, 41 death row inmates, I can honestly say that I received more than I gave, and learned more than I taught. Often, when we follow God's lead, we are better for it.

It all began in the 1980's, after I had retired from the Navy. I was at the time teaching, and giving various speeches and lectures and such, mostly about alcoholism and substance abuse. I was living in Huntington Beach in (southern) California, and I would drive to Los Angeles to teach at colleges and universities there.

I was getting tired of all of this, and a little bored and restless, so I decided to take a class myself at Golden West Junior College, one of the places where I was teaching. I wanted to fill my mind with something other than alcohol and drug abuse so I chose a Criminal Justice class which was taught one night a week, and which I came to absolutely love. There were some police officers in the class, and so I made some great friends while I earned my 'A'.

My Story

Death Row

It was toward the end of the semester that the class took a field trip to the juvenile detention facility in Chino, California, some thirty miles away. This facility housed young men between the ages of 16 and 23. I found it interesting to talk to some of the inmates there, and apparently my interest caught the attention of someone in authority there. A few weeks later one of the probation officers, Louie Perez, came to give a lecture to our Criminal Justice class. Afterword he took me aside to ask: wasn't I teaching and giving lectures on alcohol and drug abuse?

Louie, now retired and a close friend, asked if I wouldn't mind coming to Chino once a month to talk to the inmates. Of course I agreed to, and I did so for the next ten years. I became known for my work with the inmates to the extent that NBC included me in a documentary on East Los Angeles. While NBC was videotaping their documentary down there in the hood, one of the cameramen got his tripod stolen; East L.A. was –and still is– that kind of neighborhood.

One day, after I had been talking to inmates for some years, Louie called to tell me that one of the inmates I was close to had been paroled. I went to visit him and found that he was doing well, and he continued to do well, as far as I know, until he was killed in a drive-by shooting a couple of months after his release.

Marian "Pat" Benedict Cmdr. USN NC Ret.

The Silence of the Pain is Deafening

At that point I became interested in gangs and their violence and I wanted to explore the causes. I wanted to understand what it was that led young men to kill each other. I became interested in capital crime in general and its causes. Particularly, I was interested in whether alcohol or substance abuse played a role in leading someone to commit a capital crime. These thoughts continued to float in the back of my mind for some time.

I moved back to Edmond, Oklahoma (a suburb of Oklahoma City) to care for my mother in her final days, and found that my work in California followed me there in the form of a local newspaper article. Oklahoma City was experiencing an influx of youth gangs (as was much of the mid-west at that time). Someone from LA would relocate to the mid-west and recruit young men (and boys) locally, so as to be the leader of the first, and therefore the predominant gang or gang chapter in that area. The phenomenon of gangs was new to the area and many in charge were bewildered. The newspaper article identified me as an Oklahoman who had worked with law enforcement in the LA area on gang issues. As a local with knowledge about gang things, I was then sought after.

A professor teaching at Central Oklahoma State University contacted me and asked if I would come and give a talk to his class. I did, of course. It was sometime later that Louie Perez of the California Youth Authority, and Joe Guzman of the LA Sheriff's Department Gang Unit both answered my invitation to speak to the Edmond, Ok Police Department. The two came and held a seminar on gangs. In the meantime I had met and eventually became friends with Bonnie Terrell, Senior Probation and Parole Officer, Oklahoma Department of Corrections.

IN LOS ANGELES: Louie Perez, left; Joe Guzman, right
TV Commentator Linda Alvarez and myself, center

I was still giving lectures, typically one per semester per college class, at colleges in the LA area. So essentially I commuted by plane from time to time. I began to stay and teach for a semester at a time, and once, when I returned to Edmond, Oklahoma, Bonnie called and asked me if I would

The Silence of the Pain is Deafening

give a talk to a male youth group of first-time offenders at the OK State Prison in McAlester. Of course I agreed.

A local Tulsa, OK TV station did a segment on me and my work with the inmates at McAlester. The inmates were very receptive to my message and I stayed and visited with some of them after I was done speaking.

It happened that the McAlester prison is where Death Row for Oklahoma is located. After I met with the first time offenders, Bonnie and I prepared to leave. Bonnie asked me if I would like to stop by and see Death Row on our way out. That didn't sound like such a good idea to me at the time. For one thing it was absolutely pouring rain, and for another thing: why would someone want to see Death Row, anyhow? Also, I had some relatives nearby, a niece and such, whom I was anxious to go see. So at first I said, 'no thanks'.

Well, Bonnie wanted to go, and so, mostly to be sociable, I said, 'What the heck?' And so we went. Since Bonnie worked as a Parole Officer, we were allowed in. It was the most depressing place I've ever been: dank, gloomy, lonely and miserable, all I could think of was, *"I want to get out of here!"*

We didn't stay long. I said to Bonnie: "Let's get out of here." And we did.

Death Row

I'll never forget that before we left a guard said to us, "Having over 4000 Death Row inmates nationwide doesn't speak well for our society." That statement moved me.

Other Comments:

"Civilization and violence are antithetical concepts. Through violence you may murder a murderer, but you can't murder murder. Through violence you may murder a liar, but you can't establish truth. Through violence you may murder a hater, but you can't murder hate. Darkness cannot put out darkness, only light can do that."

Dr. Martin Luther King Jr.

"One is absolutely sickened, not by the crimes that the wicked have committed, but by the punishments that the good have inflicted."

Oscar Wilde

"I am constantly amazed by man's inhumanity to man."

Primo Levi

"Capital punishment would be more effective as a preventive measure if it were administered prior to the crime."

Woody Allen

"When life is holding by a thread, how expensive the price of that thread!"

Daniel Pennac

Marian "Pat" Benedict Cmdr. USN NC Ret.

The Silence of the Pain is Deafening

"An eye for an eye will make the whole world blind."

Mahatma Gandhi

"It would take me a long time to understand how systems inflict pain and hardship in people's lives and to learn that being kind in an unjust system is not enough."

Sister Helen Prejean, Dead Man Walking

"This is an execution, not surgery. Where does that come from, that you must find the method of execution that causes the least pain?"

Antonin Scalia,
US Supreme Court

My Viewpoint

Perhaps the hardest tears for us to shed are those we cause ourselves. Pain –and in particular, emotional pain– is simply part of life and unavoidable. That is, pain in life is unavoidable in a general sense, as is death, but many of us are at least somewhat responsible, both for our own pain and for the circumstances of our demise. There is pain both inside and outside of Death Row associated with the capital offenses which landed people there.

Once, when I was quite young, something prompted me to ask my mother if I was indeed her child. She responded that, although she did give birth to me, I really belonged to God,

My Story

and that I was only on loan to her. All of us will someday die; we are only on loan here on earth.

Before we point the finger or condemn another, we must remember that none on this earth are without sin. I find it interesting that, of the 41 Death Row inmates in the study, not one blamed society for his pending demise. Since the rate of capital offences differs from society to society, such that severe crimes are more characteristic of some societies than others, and since many societies do not kill offenders, one could well argue that our particular society is to blame in Death Row cases, partly for the crime committed and completely for the pending execution. That same person, born somewhere in Western Europe, might not have committed a capital offense, or having done so, would not be facing the death penalty. But the inmates I interviewed and studied, for the most part, took full responsibility for their situation.

This all brings the question, should the state take a life because an individual wrongly took a life? Does that really help the families of the crime victims in some way, or does it do little more than contribute to the social ambiance that tends to give rise to capital crimes in the first place? We, the government, can kill when we think it is right: we kill at war and we kill at home.

Marian "Pat" Benedict Cmdr. USN NC Ret.

The Silence of the Pain is Deafening

For the victims, for the inmates, I can only pray. God presides over all, and while prayer is not an answer, it is sometimes all we have; God has left things that way, so that we will reach out to Him. Prayer does no harm and it can result in much good.

Continued Concern

The guard's statement about 4000 inmates on Death Row reflecting poorly on America stayed with me over the following months and I often wondered what role alcohol and substance abuse played in the circumstances which led to those men being on Death Row. I was so moved by my short visit there that I continued to discuss Death Row with friends and acquaintances.

Finally, I decided I wanted to try actually talking to the Death Row inmates, interviewing them one on one, in an effort to determine what link, if any, might there be between alcohol and substance abuse and capital crime. I decided to approach the Oklahoma State Department of Corrections in writing.

I want to give credit to a dear friend, a fellow Oklahoman, Pete Petree, who was a great help in preparing the questionnaire which I sent with my letter. Pete was a civilian who worked in the Navy alcoholism program. Pete Petree was a longtime friend who recently passed away. At the time he was living in Yuba City, California (near Sacramento). I flew up there for a few days' stay and we brain-stormed until the questionnaire was completed.

I also needed some advice on how to proceed if and when I received permission. For that, I contacted Grayce Roessler, PHD, a nurse friend and a very smart lady. I had done some teaching for her at the Golden West Junior College. She helped me to prepare for the interviews, and also helped me to organize the results. She too has passed on and I miss her.

I sent the following letter and enclosures. While I was waiting for a response from the Department of Corrections, I began to experience second thoughts about it all. It seemed like such a good idea at first, but with continued thought, I began to doubt that the inmates would even talk to me. Also, I was spending a half a year teaching in Southern California, and so I would need to fly back and forth to my second home in Edmond, Oklahoma for interviews. There was a part of me that wouldn't have been too disappointed if the Department of Corrections had declined my request.

Marian "Pat" Benedict Cmdr. USN NC Ret.

The Silence of the Pain is Deafening

July 12, 1994

Mr. Larry Fields,
Director Oklahoma State Department of Corrections
3400 Martin Luther King
Oklahoma City, OK 73111

Dear Mr. Fields:

My name is Pat Benedict and I am a Retired Navy Nurse Commander. I am a recovering alcoholic with 21 1/2 years of sobriety. I was born and raised in Oklahoma City.

For the past 20 years I have taught and worked in the field of Chemical Dependency, having taught in the penal system for the last 16 years. I have been very involved in working with the hard core gangs by doing volunteer teaching at the California Youth Authority Training School in Chino, California since 1981. Through these experiences, I am very comfortable with and I am interested in working with incarcerated individuals and youth at risk.

In 1989 I returned to Edmond, Oklahoma from California to care for my mother who died shortly after my return. While in Oklahoma I became involved in giving seminars for Law Enforcement (CLEET) relative to gangs (which as you know were moving in from California). At our second CLEET seminar I met Sgt. Charles Casey and Cecil Young. They asked me to become involved in your S.I.P (Shock Incarceration Program), which I did do on a volunteer basis. I taught for S.I.P. on three occasions. CBS in Tulsa filmed my lecture one Saturday for a news broadcast.

The purpose of this letter is to suggest a project I would like to undertake, i.e., a series of individual informal discussions with prisoners on Death Row at McAlester State Prison

My Story

Death Row

about the effects of alcohol and drugs and the part they may have played in the lives of these people. I would like to use a questionnaire and personal interview with as many individuals as would be willing to talk with me. I am not interested in names, only the findings. I realize that not everyone would want to talk with me, some may not want to answer the questionnaire; others may want simply to talk. I think that there also may be some reasons which may preclude doing this kind of project, reasons of which I may not be aware. I have no plans at present to publish the information gathered. This would not be done in any event without your prior approval. I am simply interested in the findings.

In short, my plan would be: selection of subjects-procedures for which need to be done jointly with you, 3-4 sessions with each individual involving use of the questionnaire to gather information and serve as a basis for elaboration and discussion, and whatever follow-up with the subjects you believe should be done. I do think there should be some kind of closure for them.

Likely, a release for the meetings with each is in order-I do not know what might be required. I also do not know if any Human Subjects Review is necessary (as is required in academia). I would need your judgment on both these areas. I iterate that I do not want or need names.

My purpose for attempting to accomplish this activity is to gather as much information as possible about the role of alcohol and drugs in the lives of these people and to use my findings in work with gang members and gang deterrent projects. With information such as I hope to gather, I should have some additional persuasive data with which to get the attention of first time offenders, gang members and young

Marian "Pat" Benedict Cmdr. USN NC Ret.

people not yet in trouble and to impress on them that Death Row is a possible place that alcohol and drugs may take them. I have known several of the gang members who have been killed here in Southern California. Perhaps, with this additional information some deaths can be prevented. I realize we will likely never know but it seems worth our best efforts. There is also the possibility that a prisoner or more than one will feel that they are giving something back to society by helping to keep other youths out of prison.

As you know, changes have occurred in the State of Texas relative to incarcerated alcoholics. I have met with Governor Ann Richards of Texas, concerning the need for allocation of rehabilitation beds in Texas prisons for alcoholics and addicts. Through our efforts, laws are now in effect to address these needs. Governor Richards and I have discussed the proposal introduced in this letter; she is most interested in what we can learn from your inmates.

I am the Navy nurse who was involved in the intervention and detoxification of former First Lady Betty Ford. She continues to be deeply interested in my work. We have discussed this project and she expresses great interest in this undertaking, believing, like me, that through our continuing efforts we may be able to make a difference.

In addition, I have talked to Sgt. Carey at S.I.P. and a few of my friends in Law Enforcement here and around Oklahoma City to get a feel for how they might regard this kind of project. Also, I have taught for Professor Richard Rettig, Department of Sociology and Criminal Justice, at the University of Central Oklahoma. He has become a personal friend, among my other friends and acquaintances in law enforcement and education in the Oklahoma City area. Professor Rettig is very supportive of this proposal. We

Death Row

agree that the problems are complex, but we believe that the project is worthy of the effort. This particular approach is one that, to the best of my knowledge, has not been done before.

I am enclosing a copy of the questionnaire and my resume for your review. Please feel free to suggest changes in the questionnaire/interview guide.

I plan on coming to Tulsa the 2nd of August (next month) and would like to begin then if you are willing and able in this short lead time to give me permission to do the interviews. I will try to reach you by phone, subsequent to your receipt of this letter. I look forward to a positive response from you.

With deep appreciation for your time and consideration, I remain:
Sincerely yours,

Pat Benedict, R. N., Cdr, Navy Nurse Corps Ret.

Enc. Questionnaire/interview Guide Curriculum Vitae
cc: Ms. Mary Livers, Deputy Director, Oklahoma State Department of Corrections, Professor Richard Rettig

Marian "Pat" Benedict Cmdr. USN NC Ret.

The Silence of the Pain is Deafening

CURRICULUM VITAE

MARIAN M. (PAT) BENEDICT
Commander, U.S. Navy Nurse Corps (Retired)

Born May 12, 1930 in Oklahoma City, OK

Education:

1986   Credential
Teaching Credential, Core Curriculum for Community College, Orange Coast College, Costa Mesa, California

1975   Certificate
Alcoholism for Nurses, Psychiatric Institute Foundation, Washington DC

1974   Certificate
Basic Alcoholism Theory, US Navy Alcohol Training Center, San Diego, Calif.

1947   Diploma
St Anthony School of Nursing, Oklahoma City, OK

Licensure/Credentials:

Registered Nurse, California (Active)
Registered Nurse, Oklahoma (Active)
Register of Nurses and Midwives, Tanzania, East Africa (Expired)
Community College Limited Service Credential, Health and Physical Care Service, California

My Story

Death Row

Professional Experience:

Ongoing since
1979 Consultant, Lecturer, Interventionist
Independent Practice, Seal Beach, California.
(89 Interventions to date).

1981 Lecturer
Alcoholism and Substance Abuse, Youth Training School, California Youth Authority, Chino, California

1981 Lecturer
Gang Violence Reduction Program, California Youth Authority, East Los Angeles, California

1981 Lecturer
Alcoholism and Substance Abuse,
Continuing Education for Health Professionals
Seminar Series at Golden West College
Huntington Beach, California

1984 Associate Professor, Master's Program
Department of Social Work,
California State University, Long Beach, California

Consultancies and Lectures

1991 Consultant
Alcoholism, Substance Abuse and the Penal System, Governor Ann Richards, State of Texas

1993 Consultant/Lecturer
Defense Investigative Service, Department of Defense, Orange, California

Marian "Pat" Benedict Cmdr. USN NC Ret.

1993   Consultant/Lecturer
Great Plains Correction Prison, Hinton, Oklahoma

1992-93   Consultant/Lecturer
Council of Law Enforcement Education and Training, (C.L.E.E.T.), Law Enforcement Department, State of Oklahoma

1992-93   Consultant/Lecturer
Shock Incarceration Program (S.I.P.) for First Time Offenders, Oklahoma State Prison, McAlester, Oklahoma

1992   Lecturer
Alcoholism and Substance Abuse, Mabel Basset Correctional Center for Women, Oklahoma City, Oklahoma

1992   Consultant/Lecturer
Probation and Parole, Department of Corrections, Guthrie, Oklahoma

1992-93   Lecturer
Gangs, Department of Sociology and Criminal Justice, University of Central Oklahoma

1991-94   Consultant/Lecturer
Gang Investigation Department
Edmond Police Department, Edmond, Oklahoma

1985   Lecturer
N.A.S.A, U. S. Air Force, El Segundo, California
1983 Presenter, "Alcohol and Substance Abuse," World Federation for Mental Health Congress, Washington, D.C.

1982   Lecturer
Alcohol and Substance Abuse, FAA Air Traffic Controller School, Oklahoma City, Oklahoma

Death Row

1980-89　　Lecturer
Alcoholism and Substance Abuse Starting Point
Costa Mesa, CA

1980　　Lecturer
Alcohol and Substance Abuse, The Friary
Gulf Breeze, Florida

1979-88　　Lecturer
Alcoholism and Substance Abuse Treatment Centers, Tustin Community Hospital, Tustin, California; St. Joseph Hospital, Orange, California; and Care Unit, Orange, California

1978-79　　Lecturer
Alcohol and Substance Abuse, Navy Airbase, Pensacola, Florida

1978　　Lecturer
Alcoholism and Substance Abuse, Tinker Air Force Base, Oklahoma City, Oklahoma

1975-88　　Lecturer
Delinquency Control Institute and Police Administration Institute, School of Public Administration, University of Southern California, Los Angeles, California

1974-89　　Lecturer
Alcoholism Outpatient Department, San Pedro Peninsula Hospital, San Pedro, California

Marian "Pat" Benedict Cmdr. USN NC Ret.

Military Service

1974-79	US Naval Hospital, Long Beach, Calif.
1969-73	US Naval Hospital, Newport, RI
1969-69	US Naval Hospital, San Diego, Calif.
1965-67	USS Repose, Hospital Ship Republic of South Vietnam
1962-65	US Naval Hospital, Bethesda, MD
1960-62	Staff Nurse, OB-GYN, St Anthony Hospital Oklahoma City, OK
1958-60	Lay Medical Missionary in Tanzania, East Africa for Archdiocese of Los Angeles
1957-58	US Naval Hospital, Corpus Christi, TX
1956-57	U.S. Naval Hospital, Corona, California
1952-54	U.S. Navy Hospital, Bainbridge, Maryland
1951-52	U.S. Naval Hospital, St. Albans, New York

Special Areas of Expertise:

Alcoholism and Substance Abuse, addiction, intervention and treatment, medical aspects; Female alcoholics and addicts; alcoholism and addiction in nurses and physicians; family violence, incest, sexual dysfunction, family dynamics, codependency, and other aspects; Gangs: gang membership and activities, interventions, alcohol and substance abuse, ethnic gangs, gangs in the military, female gangs, and other aspects

Community/Professional Activities:

Co-Founder
Nurses Diversion Program, Board of Registered Nursing, State of California
Former Chairperson
Impaired Nurses Diversion Program, Board of Registered Nursing, State of California

Lecturer
Continuing Education credit seminars for nurses and other health professionals on Alcoholism and Substance Abuse (ongoing)
Former Liaison
National Nurses Society on Alcoholism and the American Medical Society on Alcoholism
Camp Nurse
Gang Deterrent Camp, San Bernardino Mountains, sponsored by the California Youth Authority, Los Angeles Sheriff Department, California Highway Patrol, Los Angeles Police Department, (ongoing)
Volunteer
Working on Skid Row, Los Angeles, California
Volunteer counselor
Youth Training School, California Youth Authority, Chino, Calif.

Professional Associations/Societies:

U.S. Navy Nurse Corps Association
California Association of Alcoholism Counselors
California Association of Nurses Substance Abuse
National Nurses Society on Alcoholism
Transcultural Nursing Society
American Legion, Life Member
Disabled American Veterans, Life Member
Veterans of Foreign Wars, Life Member

Honors and Awards, Military:

1979 Commendation Medal for Work in the Field of Alcoholism, United States Navy
1978 Certificate of Commendation for Teaching, Alcoholism and Substance Abuse,

1975-78 Conferred by Commandant, United States Marine Corps, El Toro, California
1966 Vietnam Service Medal
1966 Vietnam Defense Campaign
1966 Counter-Offensive Campaign, Phase II
1966 "Gallantry Cross," Armed Forces Meritorious Unit Citation, Republic of Vietnam 1966 National Defense Medal with Star
1965 Unit Citation, United States Navy

Honors and Awards, Civilian:

1993 Letter of Appreciation for Service
Gang Intelligence Division, Edmond Police Department, Edmond, Oklahoma
1993 Profiled by CBS News, Tulsa, Oklahoma, concerning work with the Shock Incarceration Program for First Offenders, Oklahoma State Prison, McAlester, Oklahoma
1992 Profiled by NBC News, Los Angeles in series on Gangs
July 1994 Distinguished Service Award, California Youth Authority, Chino, Calif.

Death Row

Cdr. Pat Benedict,
US Navy Nurse Corps, Ret.

Questionnaire / Interview Guide

Do you have a history of substance abuse (alcohol and/or drugs)? (circle one) Y N

Age at which you started drinking: _____

Age at which you started using: _____
Choice of drugs: _____

Do you feel you are an alcoholic? Y N

Do you feel you are an addict? Y N

Have you experienced any blackouts? Y N

Have you ever been confronted about your alcohol or drug abuse? Y N

Did you experience any personality changes when drinking or using drugs? Y N
If yes, check one or more:
Happy___   Mellow___   Aggressive___   Depressed___

Have you experienced any loss of control of your drinking once you started drinking? Y N

Did you experience any remorse or guilt after heavy drinking or using drugs? Y N

Have you had any drunk driving convictions? Y N
How many? _____

Marian "Pat" Benedict Cmdr. USN NC Ret.

The Silence of the Pain is Deafening

Have you ever been treated for alcohol or drug use? Y N

Were you an inpatient? How many days? _____
Outpatient days: _____

Are you a veteran? Y N
Branch of service: _____
Years of service: _____

Were you honorably discharged? Y N

Did you serve in Vietnam? Y N

Did you come from an abusive home? Y N

Do you or did you belong to a gang? Y N

Do you feel alcohol and drug(s) played a part in your criminal behavior? Y N

Did you ever have withdrawals from alcohol or drugs? Y N

Did you ever become addicted to prescription med's? Y N

Have you ever been arrested for being drunk or for disorderly conduct? Y N

Have you experienced any health problems due to alcohol or drug use? Y N

Have you ever lost a job due to alcohol or drug use? Y N

Are you a high school graduate? Y N
If not, what grade did you complete? _____

My Story

Death Row

Did you attend college? Y N
How many years? _____

Did you ever attend Alcoholic Anonymous or Narcotics / Cocaine Anonymous? Y N

Have you ever overdosed? Y N
If yes, on what drug? _____

Were you a marijuana smoker? Y N
If yes, at what age and how often? _____

List all of the drugs you have used or experienced: _____
_____
_____

Have you experienced any sexual dysfunction while drinking or using drugs? Y N

Have you ever attempted suicide while under the influence of drugs or alcohol? Y/N

What was your pattern of drinking or using (daily, weekends, occasionally, etc.)? _____

Did you ever abuse your children physically, emotionally or sexually while under the influence of drugs or alcohol? Y N

Were you abused as a child in your home, physically, emotionally or sexually? Y N

Have you ever been sexually abused? Y N

Have you ever been treated for a psychiatric disorder? Y N
What and when? _____

Marian "Pat" Benedict Cmdr. USN NC Ret.

The Silence of the Pain is Deafening

Your age: _____

Age at which you were first arrested: _____

Age at which you were first incarcerated: _____

Age at which you came on Death Row: _____

Present marital status: Single ___ Married ___ Divorced ___ Widower ___

How many times have you been married? ___ Divorced? ___

Income range before incarceration: _____

Ethnicity: White ___ Black ___ Hispanic ___ Asian ___ Native American ___
Other or mixed: _____

Religious affiliation: _____

My Story

Death Row

Dept. of Corrections Replies

Over the next six weeks or so I received two letters in reply to the above letter and enclosures. The first was from James Saffle, director of the southeast region of the Oklahoma Department of Corrections.

The Silence of the Pain is Deafening

August 8, 1994

Pat Benedict, R. N., Cmdr., Navy Nurse Corps Ret.
13601 Del Monte Dr. 55A
Seal Beach, California 90740

Dear Commander Benedict:

I have reviewed your correspondence addressed to Director Fields, and since the Shock Incarceration Unit is at the Oklahoma State Penitentiary, your correspondence was referred to me for a response.

Since you express a desire to hold informal discussions with inmates on Death Row, I am forwarding your correspondence to Warden Reynolds. Warden Reynolds will need to review your request and determine if he can adequately honor your request as stated.

Warden Reynolds will respond to your request and if approved, he will be the authority on coordinating scheduling. I would recommend that you deal with him directly.

We do appreciate your interest in the Oklahoma Department of Corrections.

Sincerely,

James L. Saffle,
Regional Director Southeastern Region
copy: Director Larry A. Fields
Warden Dan M. Reynolds, Oklahoma State Penitentiary

My Story

Death Row

The second letter came from Dan Reynolds, the Warden overseeing Death Row.

August 23, 1994

Pat Benedict, RN, Cmdr., Navy Nurse Corp, Ret.
13601 Del Monte Dr. 55A
Seal Beach, CA 90740

Dear Commander Benedict:

In response to your request to conduct a project on Death Row at Oklahoma State Penitentiary, please be advised that the project has been approved by the Research and Evaluation Department at the Department of Corrections.

I can advise that, in the past, Death Row offenders have not been receptive to participation in such projects. Upon advice of legal counsel, the offenders have declined to participate in completing questionnaires, or discussing their past lives with persons outside the facility. The promise of anonymity seems to have no bearing on their decision.

Please advise the facility when you are ready to implement the project.
If I can be of assistance, please contact me.
Sincerely,

Dan M. Reynolds, Warden
Oklahoma State Penitentiary
Cc: James L. Saffle, Regional Director

Marian "Pat" Benedict Cmdr. USN NC Ret.

The Silence of the Pain is Deafening

So there it was: my response from the Oklahoma Dept. of Corrections. They said yes, that the warden and staff at Death Row were expecting to hear from me and so there was no turning back. I contacted the warden's office, where I talked to Lee Mann, his assistant. I made the arrangements with her to come there to work out the details of my interviews.

I stayed with my niece who lived nearby and who was nice enough to drive me there. When we arrived at the McAlester Correctional Center it was pouring rain, as it had been when Bonnie and I had gone there. I suggested to my niece that this might be an omen.

I spent a couple of hours with Lee Mann, the warden's assistant, who was very nice and helpful, and I met with the warden. They also emphasized verbally that others have tried to interview inmates. Death Row inmates typically refuse to be interviewed, sometimes on the advice of attorneys, sometimes just according to their own attitudes, but others have tried without success. I replied that I thought that the inmates would talk to me. I thought I had a few things going for me: being female, a nurse, a Vietnam veteran and myself a recovering alcoholic. Also, this would not be my first time with inmates, only my first time talking to Death Row residents. I worked out all the details. I would stay in a nearby motel and, starting in April of 1995, I would conduct interviews. I did so for the next three years, until July of 1998.

I interviewed about five inmates a day. There was quite a procedure involved in bringing each inmate for the interview. The inmate would first be strip-searched in his cell and then allowed to dress. He would be brought down for the interview with his hands chained to his sides and his legs in chains. We would then meet face to face (or you could say knee to knee). The inmate would sign the paperwork when the interview was over (usually an hour or two later). Afterward I would wait in the office for the inmate to be returned and another to be brought out.

I would always send a thank you note to each one when I got back. The warden said the inmates were thrilled to get them; for some that was the only mail they ever got.

On one morning I cancelled an appointment at the Social Security office in downtown Oklahoma City so I could get some more interviews done. The atmosphere was tense when I arrived at the prison, and the guards were all carrying shotguns. I asked what had happened and I was told that the federal building in Oklahoma City had just been blown up. That was where I would have been if I hadn't cancelled: at the Social Security office on the first floor. I quickly made some phone calls to family members who knew I was supposed to

Marian "Pat" Benedict Cmdr. USN NC Ret.

be at that building at that time, to assure them that I was OK. (Thank you, Lord –ed.)

The Death Row inmates were allowed some arts and crafts supplies (not scissors or knives of course). One inmate, Eagle Clayton, made four beautiful Indian paintings for me, which are hanging in my home.

Jeff Matthews had learned from his grandmother how to sew and knit. I sent a money order to the warden for supplies and reimbursed the Chaplain, who mailed the bears to me for distribution to sick and dying children.

LWER PAT BENEDICT (photo above) distributes stuffed animals handmade by an Oklahoma death-row inmate to ill children. Crocheted teddy bears are dressed in hats and vests.

Leisure World Connection
Inmate's kindness benefits children
by Cathie Merz
section editor

"You can take away our names and replace them with numbers, cage and store us in conditions not even fit for your family dog, and exterminate us at your whim, but we are still

Death Row

human beings, capable of everything from love and beauty to violence and hate."

Thomas B. Whitaker
Texas Death Row inmate #999522

The above pictured bears were made by Jeffery. He didn't tell me about his bear hobby during the interview; I found out a few months later when I corresponded with him by mail. He insisted that the bears go to sick and dying young children. He didn't want anyone to know where they came from and he didn't want to be thanked by anyone. This was just something he wanted to do for the children.

Marian "Pat" Benedict Cmdr. USN NC Ret.

The Silence of the Pain is Deafening

We eventually made arrangements with a minister in McAlester. I covered the postage and packaging costs and he boxed them up and sent them out.

Marian "Pat" Benedict with teddy bears for paralyzed veterans (photo above). Death row inmate Jeffrey Matthews made stuffed animals (photo below) that Ms. Benedict will deliver to children on the cancer ward of Long Beach Memorial Medical Center.

Veteran to Veteran

'Beary' Special Delivery

by Ruth Osborn
staff writer

"I can give them each a teddy and a hug. I'm going to give them out Friday," said Pat.

Marian "Pat" Benedict of

Just before his execution Jeffery sent a letter, apologizing for not getting around to making a bear for me. I sent him a letter saying that there were two bears left over but he was executed before the letter arrived. A 21 year old marine was checked into Long Beach VA Hospital, paralyzed from the neck down. I contacted his father and he agreed that his son would probably like one of the bears so I brought the red, white and blue one and set it on his chest. He was quite pleased.

My Story

Death Row

Inmate Robert Brecheen was very helpful in getting other inmates to be interviewed. More on him later

Interview Results

For the racial makeup of the interviewees, 42 of those questioned responded; 28 identified themselves as White, 11 as Black, one identified himself as Hispanic one as Mexican-Indian and one as racially mixed. Forty-two also responded to the question about age. The ages ranged from 21 to 45, with half of the respondents being in their thirties.

Geographical Backgrounds

Thirty one Death Row inmates responded to the question about their birthplace; about a third were born in Oklahoma, a few in Texas and the rest were from a variety of states.

The Silence of the Pain is Deafening

Twenty-eight responded to the question about where they were raised, and less than half said they were raised in Oklahoma, with more than a fourth claiming California as the location of their upbringing. The rest of the locations were scattered across the US. Twenty of the thirty inmates who responded to the question of who raised them said that they were raised by one or both biological parents; the other ten were raised by extended family members, foster parents or others.

Gangs

Forty-three inmates responded to the question about gang affiliation; 16 affirmed and 27 said no. Some identified themselves with the Crips or the Bloods, two mostly black youth gangs from California. Other affiliations given included motorcycle gangs, the KKK and the American Nazi Party, as well as prison gangs.

Education

Fifteen said they graduated from high school; 26 said they did not. Three said they did not go past the sixth grade; three claimed the eighth as their highest grade level; the remaining twenty non-grads dropped out sometime during high school. Most of the inmates had children. Two-thirds of those with children said that they had helped to raise their children.

My Story

Death Row

Abuse Victims

Two thirds said they came from an abusive home. Three said they were sexually abused at home, while more than a third said they had been sexually abused at some point in their lives (probably while in jail or prison). Half of the respondents reported having immediate family members who were then, or who had been jailed or imprisoned.

Substance Abuse

Twenty-nine inmates responded to questions about substance abuse. Of those, more than a third had started drinking before they were ten years old; more than a third said they had used marijuana by the age of 7; <u>nearly all</u> Death Row inmates reported having sniffed glue, or abused drugs and/ or alcohol <u>by their mid-teens</u>. For comparison purposes, note that in a Center for Disease Control survey conducted from 1999 to 2004, less than half of all Americans aged 12-17 had tried alcohol, three fourths had never tried marijuana and about 98% had never tried any cocaine product.

Drugs of Choice

Marijuana was preferred over all other drugs by the largest number of respondents, while a little over half that many favored amphetamines, followed close behind by cocaine and then alcohol. Among those Death Row inmates who had used alcohol, narcotics or cocaine, roughly half admitted to being addicted. The CDC reports that in their most recent survey only 9.4% of Americans aged 12 or older said they had used an illicit drug during the previous month.

Limits

Of course, with a survey of this sort it cannot be determined whether drug use led to the commission of a capital crime, or whether the same factors which led to drug use also led to severe anti-social behaviors such as aggravated murder. One might reasonably judge that both is the case. We can imagine that a troubled youth who was inclined to comfort his psyche with illicit drugs, glue sniffing and/or alcohol at an early age, and who dropped out of the discipline of school during or even prior to adolescence, would likely suffer from impaired thought processes and judgement, and would also not be inclined to obey the rules of society.

Our government has tried cracking down on illicit drugs for many decades with little success. Perhaps treating drug and alcohol abuse as symptoms of mental or emotional problems and intervening in the lives of troubled children at the earliest sign of such problems would be a more successful approach.

"Almost all of my [Death Penalty] clients should have been taken out of their homes when they were children. They weren't. Nobody had any interest in them until, as a result of

My Story

nobody's interest in them, they became menaces, at which point society did become interested, if only to kill them."

David R. Dow
Texas Public Defender Service attorney

Robert Brecheen

The first Death Row inmate I want to share with you is Robert Brecheen. Robert stands out among the inmates I met for a number of reasons. The more I got to know him the more I thought, *"This man does not belong on death row."* Not because of his crime (although other men here and in other states convicted of similar crimes were eventually released on parole) but because of what sort of man he was.

I'll start with his questionnaire. Robert had no history of illegal drug use or even alcohol abuse. He did not take his first drink until age 23 and he limited his drinking to a moderate level and only on weekends. He wasn't affiliated with any sort of gang and hadn't been in trouble (not even a traffic ticket) before. For some reason Robert never discussed his crime with me. Robert grew up in a non-abusive household among two brothers and six sisters; he was a Christian believer and was somewhat active in his church (Baptist) during his childhood and teen years.

The Silence of the Pain is Deafening

Robert was a trustee on Death Row and was thus allowed out of his cell to deliver meals and things to other inmates. He was the first inmate I interviewed and without his help I might not have had much success in my project there at the Oklahoma Death Row. I think maybe God was working through Robert. I wasn't the only one he helped; there was an inmate known as 'Pinky' who was too old to care for himself. Robert was happy to have the opportunity to help Pinky and eventually Pinky's bed was moved into Robert's cell so that Robert could feed him, bathe him and change his bedding.

Pinky wasn't executed; rather he died in the prison infirmary while awaiting an appeal of his case. Robert, too, nearly died before his execution; more on that later.

Robert's was the first of my Death Row interviews. The supervising officer sat me down and offered me a cup of coffee while a correctional officer went to get Robert. As a trustee, he was the easiest inmate to bring to the interview. His first words to me were, "What can I do for you?" In his case, that was a sincere question. I think Robert was happiest when helping others and he was quite eager to help me. He said of my project that it was a good thing, even if it helped only one person.

Robert and I became friends from the start; we found we could make each other laugh easily. I handed him a copy of the questionnaire and asked if he could possibly get me some volunteers to be interviewed.

Robert smiled and said, "I'll give this project my very best salesmanship talk." Robert was gone about an hour. He returned with a triumphant grin and said, "I got you 45 guys who will talk with you."

I met Robert's mother and two of his sisters. I asked his sister, Loyce Freeman, to write to me about Robert's last day of freedom. I want to share with you what she wrote.

From Loyce Freeman

Well I had a few moments and I told you I would write a little about Robert...

Pat, all I know is that Randy, Bennie, Joyce and I were over at mother's on a Sunday. Randy and I were needing some garage doors and so the men decided to go to Sherman, Texas. Since Robert was there, they asked him if he would like to go and he said sure, that he just got paid and that he wanted to get some cement blocks for Sherry's trailer. We

The Silence of the Pain is Deafening

just happened to see in the paper where they had garage doors very reasonable so we borrowed momma and daddy's trailer and the men left. They were back about 6:30 pm because I told them a new show was going to come on and it was the Thorn Birds, which I never got to watch in all these years, but anyway it was putting us late in getting home. Robert laughed and told Randy that you better get Loyce home cause she has been waiting since the advertisement of that show to watch it. Randy and Bennie and Robert all came in mother's house and Robert said well it doesn't look like you and Randy are going to get Loyce home in time for the show to start cause the minute they came in I was hurrying Randy out the door to watch the show.

Robert said, "One thing about TVs you can catch it on reruns."

I just kept on telling Randy 'Let's go'. Robert went to the stove and got him something to eat cause the kitchen and the living room were all connected so Robert got him a plate fixed and was in the process of eating when daddy called him to help him up cause daddy had had hernia surgery and had caught staph which made him weak and daddy like to have died. I still kinda blame myself cause daddy asked me if he should have it and I said well you need to go ahead before

Death Row

retirement age and then he liked to have died from it. Daddy told me later in the hospital he should never have listened to me, which I knew daddy was sick and it was the medicine talking. But back to Robert: he was headed to daddy's room when we all left.

All I can remember about that night is around 11:00 pm I got a phone call from momma saying Robert had been shot and she did not know his condition. So I headed over to the hospital and the DA was outside Robert's room. They let me in to see him and Robert was kinda out of it. I told him they said a woman had been killed.

And Pat, he said, "Oh my God; I killed her!"

I talked to the DA and he asked me questions like did Robert have any enemies. I said no and he asked was Robert under any financial stress and I said he has a job and he just got paid. After the trial was over I got Robert's wallet and there was 500 dollars in it and when we got the money out to finish paying the lawyer there was blood all over it and I got sick and I don't know how blood got all over it or what happened to the wallet.

But I told the DA that Robert was about to get married and that he had been in Sherman and that he got cement blocks

Marian "Pat" Benedict Cmdr. USN NC Ret.

for their trailer and we had gotten garage doors and that was all he asked me.

The rest of the family got there and they transported Robert to the city but the doctors told me that he has lost the use of his right arm and they had to send him to a neurologist but that he would probably have to have a brace on to help him with the movement of his arm so this is about all I know.

I loved Robert and I still do and I think about him often. Not hardly a day goes by that I don't think about him. This has been the hardest thing in my life I have had to face. I still struggle with it at times but my faith in God keeps me going and I will someday get to see him and it won't matter anymore.

If you have any more questions I will do my best to answer them. I love ya.

Loyce

There are some statements by Robert at the end of his questionnaire which offer a clue about what happened.

Question: What would you tell kids if you had the opportunity?

Robert's answer: Stop and think what you are doing to yourself– be responsible or the prison will be responsible– fear will make you make the worst mistakes of your life–

Death Row

Now when I met with Robert's sisters, and when I met his mother, each of them said that Robert never talked about what he did or why. And I myself never asked him.

According to a Mr. Hilton Stubbs, he woke up to hear his wife scream in the living room of their home. He looked out of the bedroom, heard a gunshot and saw his wife fall to the floor. As Robert approached the bedroom, Mr. Stubbs grabbed his gun and rolled off of the bed onto the floor. Robert then fired into the empty bed and Mr. Stubbs returned fire, hitting Robert, who ran toward the front door. Mr. Stubbs fired again and Robert stopped at the front door and fired back before running out.

According to the State of Oklahoma, Robert had entered the home without permission, for the purpose of theft. A jury convicted Robert of murder and burglary. He was sentenced to death for the murder and to 20 years for the burglary. Robert spent 12 years on Death Row, during the appeals process.

Note that sometimes a prosecutor will threaten to 'throw the book at' a defendant while offering a lesser plea in exchange for testimony against someone else. Certainly Robert's sister Loyce loved him unconditionally; it could be that he never talked –even to her– about what happened or why because he was protecting someone –perhaps his fiancé or a friend.

Marian "Pat" Benedict Cmdr. USN NC Ret.

The Silence of the Pain is Deafening

I saw Robert one last time before his execution. I was invited to speak in Dublin, Ireland at the World Federation of Mental Health. Robert's execution was scheduled to take place while I was in Ireland; a final appeal to the Supreme Court was all that stood in the way.

I asked Robert if he wanted me to stay with him and skip the trip to Ireland. He said no, no; you go ahead; I'm sure you'll do some good there, and I saw that he seemed to be at peace within himself. We were able to hold hands briefly –we shook hands actually– I could just reach him through the bars. I took the opportunity of our last face to face meet to tell Robert that he probably saved my life. I was referring to the time when I had an appointment to be at the Social Security office in the Alfred P. Murrah Federal Building in Oklahoma City. I had so many inmates to interview (thanks to Robert) that instead of keeping my appointment I decided to get caught up on my interviews. That was the day of the famous Oklahoma City Bombing, which killed many of the people who were in that Social Security office at the time (including a friend of mine).

Robert and I exchanged further pleasantries, and of course I took the opportunity to thank Robert profusely. He was such a kind-hearted and helpful soul. He had said that if he could have done anything he wanted with his life he would have been a social worker, and I certainly have no reason to doubt his sincerity in that.

Well, I went to Ireland. Among the things I was speaking on was the death penalty (ironically enough) and of course Robert was in the back of my mind the whole time.

In the United Kingdom, as in most developed countries, they do not execute criminals, and many of the people there are appalled that we in America sometimes do. News of Robert's execution came to me from the front page of the newspaper there in Dublin, Ireland. The article was by Reuters, entitled:

Prisoner revived and then executed in US.

I read: *"US prison officials revived a condemned killer who apparently overdosed on drugs before his execution and then put him to death several hours later with a lethal injection, officials said yesterday.*

Robert Brecheen (40) was executed at the Oklahoma State Penitentiary for killing a woman in an attempted robbery in 1983.

His last appeal before the US Supreme Court was rejected on Thursday and, three hours before the scheduled execution, he was found unconscious, apparently from a drug overdose, a spokesman for the Oklahoma Department of Corrections said.

Marian "Pat" Benedict Cmdr. USN NC Ret.

The Silence of the Pain is Deafening

He was brought to hospital, revived and returned to prison for the execution."

The article went on to say that the law in Oklahoma requires that the condemned person be coherent enough to know what is happening to him for the execution to proceed. The officials stated that he was sufficiently coherent for a legal execution, while one of Robert's lawyers said that he was not.

I wanted to include the legal history of the end of Robert's life, starting with the crime. On March 27, 1983, Marie Stubbs, 59, was shot in the head and killed in her home in Ardmore, Oklahoma. Also, Robert Brecheen, 28, of Milo, OK, was shot by Marie's husband, Hilton Stubbs, 58.

Robert Brecheen was found lying in his truck a block away from the Stubbs' home after an investigator followed a trail of blood. He was arrested and taken to a hospital.

On April 4, 1983, Robert was denied bail and on June 8 he was bound over for trial on charges of first degree murder and first degree burglary.

The first time ever that a Carter County jury recommended the death penalty was on August 30 of 1983, after Robert was convicted on both charges. They also recommended a 20 year sentence for the burglary charge.

A judge followed the jury's recommendation. On Sept. 29, 1983 he sentenced Robert Brecheen to death and sentenced him to 20 years for the burglary charge. He also denied a motion for a new trial. Robert's execution date was set for December 27 of 1983.

A stay of execution pending appeals was later granted and then, two years later, on December 19 of 1985, an appeals court ordered an evidentiary hearing because the trial court refused to consider evidence of jury misconduct during the motion for a new trial.

On February 20, 1986, a trial court found that there was no evidence of juror misconduct, and then, 11 months later, on January 27 of 1987, a State Court of Appeals confirmed the trial court finding of no evidence of juror misconduct.

Seven and a half years later, on July 1, 1994, a US Appeals Court granted an emergency request for a stay of execution, pending further appeals. On October 14, 1994, the 10th Circuit Court of Appeals voted 2 to 1 not to overturn Robert's conviction or death sentence.

Eight months later, on June 5 of 1995, an execution date of August 11 was set. On July 31, clemency was denied by the Oklahoma State Pardon and Parole board. On August 2nd and 3rd motions were filed to stay the execution pending further appeals. On Thursday, August 10, the US Supreme Court declined to review the case and in the early morning hours of

The Silence of the Pain is Deafening

Friday, August 11, 1995 Robert Brecheen was resuscitated from a drug overdose and then executed.

Sean Sellers

Sean also stands out among the many Death Row inmates I interviewed over the three year period. He was arrested once in his life, at the age of 16, when he was arrested for murder.

An Associated Press article said that "even as he was taking his final breath" his "words still managed to anger his family." But he was really just behaving like a Christian, there on his death bed.

After his execution, his stepsister, Noelle Terry was quoted in a Wikipedia article and by the Associated Press as saying, "It made me very angry." She went on to say, "He took his last dig at us. He basically addressed the fact that we would still feel the same. It's very presumptuous that he would know how we would still feel." Other family members also expressed anger toward Sean after his death.

What he did, according to online sources, was to call out the first names of each of the members of the Bellofatto family, those who were there to see him die for killing Paul Bellofatto, his stepfather. He then addressed "all of the people who are hating me right now and are here waiting to see me die." He told them, "When you wake up tomorrow you aren't going to feel any different."

Sean Sellers said, "You are going to hate me as much tomorrow as you do tonight. When you wake up and nothing has changed inside, reach out to God and He will be there for you. Reach out to God and He will hear you. Let Him touch your hearts. Don't hate all your lives."

From a Christian perspective, one can be enslaved to anger, hatred and vengeance. Acting out these ill feelings does not free a person from them; only God can do that, and sometimes He does that when a person is regenerated or 'born again.' It is not unusual for someone (like Sean) who has been freed from ill feelings, at least to some extent, by God, to urge others to reach out to God for relief, not unlike someone, having jumped into a pool on a particularly hot day, saying to others, "Come on in; it feels great!" By all appearances, Sean, on his death bed, was genuinely concerned for the mental, emotional and spiritual wellbeing of those who hated him the most, those who hungered for his death and objected to any clemency or lesser sentence.

According to online sources, Sean then spoke the names of each of the seven witnesses who were there on his behalf, saying kind things, before telling them, "I love you all." He laid back down, looked straight up and said loudly: "Here I come, Father. I'm coming home." He then turned to Warden Gary Gibson and said, "Let's do it, Gary; let's get it on." Sean then sang "Set my spirit free that I might praise Thee. Set my spirit free that I might worship Thee," while his execution proceeded, until the drugs took effect. Those were his last words.

Sean had spent some ten years on Death Row, receiving some therapy while being housed during the long appeals process. The very angry, drug-tainted 16 year old Satanist who murdered his mother and stepfather had apparently changed, despite his living conditions. One could imagine that, after five or perhaps ten years of therapy and other treatments in a better environment, he would have become a productive citizen, had he been treated and then released. Very few governments on earth will put someone to death for a crime committed as a sixteen year old. Indeed our Supreme Court found five years later in another case that it is unconstitutional to execute someone for a crime committed while under the age of 18. One appeals court did find that Sean probably was legally insane at the time he committed the crimes, and while the jury at his trial had not been told of his mental health problems, the insanity defense was submitted too late in the appeals process to be considered. Human Rights Watch condemned the decision to deny the insanity defense "on narrow procedural grounds."

My Story

Death Row

Human Rights Watch also wrote to Oklahoma's governor, saying that "no civilized society can accept the execution of a person who was a child at the time he committed his crimes and who was -- and remains -- afflicted with a mental disorder. Such an execution offends the most basic principles of international justice and morality." Sean used methamphetamine and was a worshipper of Satan when the crimes were committed. His conversion to Christianity came while in prison. In his questionnaire he stated that he had wanted to become a Christian when he was 13 but that he didn't know how, and so he turned to Satanism. He stated that he had been abused physically and emotionally by his mother; also sexually. Every time I talked to Sean he told me to urge kids to stay away from satanic rituals and Satanism. He felt that Satanism, more than drug use, led to his crimes.

Here is something Sean Sellers wrote, mostly to God, as he faced the end of his life. Here he decried the masks that we all wear to hide our true inner selves from one another so that we can get along. Such masks won't be necessary in heaven.

Naked Before You

In a world of plastic and makeup, where only actors survive, I hide my secrets and feelings beneath a mask to stay alive.

Marian "Pat" Benedict Cmdr. USN NC Ret.

The Silence of the Pain is Deafening

I can never allow anyone to know how weak I am inside, and how sometimes when things get rough, I only want to hide. And as I open up my closet, to choose the mask of the day, I wear my disguises upon my knees before You as I pray.

But the person I see in the mirror, knows only pain and strife, and if people only knew the despairing thoughts that roam my mind, perhaps they would understand how their pride in me is so unkind.

But how do I explain to them what they see is so unreal, when the masks they wear themselves hide from me what they feel? All around me are plastic people who carry the Name of God. If there was one who was real, perhaps it wouldn't be so hard.

I gather up my costume, a jacket and a plastic mask, with a painted on smile, and broken limbs within a cast. But only outward do I smile for it covers over what I hide. All these things that must not be seen; anger, envy and pride.

But it makes no matter how I try, no matter the disguise I wear. For the tears drip beneath the mask, and the jacket has a tear. I pray for strength to let it loose, to give up all I hold. To walk in life free and real, open, unashamed and bold.

I know You would give more than You ever take away. And I'd lay before Your Feet, the souls of others as I pray. Now

My Story

Death Row

today as I arose and opened up the closet door, I found all my disguises, lying broken on the floor.

I tried to mend the ones I could, ashamed for You to see. I had not truly been all I claimed to be.

Finally I put together, one last costume of my choice, and cautiously, lest it tear, I knelt beside my chair. But it began to tighten as I listened to Your Voice. And revealed the shape of sin that You always knew was there.

And when at last I could not breathe, nor find fake words to say, I stuck my hands to my bare chest and ripped all else away.

So now I'm trying something new, and can only say I'm scared. No longer can I wear the masks nor jackets I once dared. You deserve all of me, and there is no part I can hide. I've shown You many costumes, now dear God please look inside. With nothing to hide me anymore from Your view, at last God here I stand, naked before You.

This is me You've created, the me that You deserve. And from now on my Lord, this is how I'll serve. Let people laugh and jeer and sneer, at every blemish that's now clear. I'd endure this naked realness Lord, more than clothing mad of fear. And should plastic people follow, with courage to

Marian "Pat" Benedict Cmdr. USN NC Ret.

undress, there will be no shame beside me, embraced in nakedness.

Media Attention

Sean's story drew the attention of mass media. He appeared on The Oprah Winfrey Show and in a Geraldo segment about Satanism, as well as in documentaries concerning Satanism and crime on 48 Hours, MSNBC and the A&E Network.

As Sean's execution approached, many spoke out against it, including Archbishop Desmond Tutu, the American Bar Association and the European Union.

Most countries in the world have signed the International Covenant on Civil and Political Rights, which forbids the execution of anyone for crimes committed while under the age of 18. Our congress ratified the treaty, with the exception of the part about executing juveniles. The Convention on the Rights of the Child also forbids such executions, but America is one of the few countries which failed to ratify that treaty.

Introspection

I was criticized by several people for doing my Death Row study. I don't mind the criticism and I understand that some people would rather not deal with the ugly side of life. Some would avoid talking about war just because it is an unpleasant subject. I learned a lot about pain, suffering, sadness and the loss of innocent life in Vietnam. To write about Vietnam, to

Death Row

write about what I saw and felt, was a cleansing experience for me. It helped me to put the memories in a more comfortable place in my mind.

My experience in interviewing Death Row inmates had the effect of enhancing the way I value life. I don't understand the taking of one human life by another human, whether as a crime or as state-sponsored retribution. But I learned from those men on Death Row, those men who dealt in death and are facing death; I learned to love life as the only thing that we really have of our own.

Whatever else you, the reader may gather from my work on Death Row, I hope you give some thought to the taking of life whether as a personal act, as a form of law enforcement or in war, for whatever reason.

Marian "Pat" Benedict Cmdr. USN NC Ret.

Epilogue

Catharsis

Producing this work –call it an autobiography, call it a memoir– producing this accounting, this record of my life has been cathartic. I have laughed and cried, and I have experienced an inner freedom, a release.

In a way alcoholism was the best thing that happened to me. In a way it was for the best because of what I gained in recovery. I learned to be more forgiving, for one thing, for which I am grateful. Also I learned to be more honest with myself and to 'clean up my side of the street,' as they say. Mistakes are part of life for humans, and I learned to accept mine and those of other people. Being more accepting of myself has allowed me to look within and understand myself and to do some housekeeping, to improve myself.

Preparing this work has helped me to put Vietnam behind me (after 50 years!). It has helped me to get in touch with my feelings, to come to terms with them and to put it all to rest within myself. My future is in front of me and this final look back will be helping me to look forward.

My good friend Bill Hunnicutt (now deceased) used to say "Alcoholics Anonymous is a language of the heart." And yes, indeed it is.

Epilogue

My Editor

To my dear and close cousin, Steve Keller, who edited this work, and who has hung in with me for many, many months, there are no words to thank you– but my deepest love you will have forever– you have done a tremendous job– my gratitude and love you will have always– and for every bit of work and effort "I salute you"!

Marian "Pat" Benedict Cmdr. USN NC Ret.

Distinguished Service Award

presented to

Pat Benedict

In Recognition of Dedicated Service

to

The Department of the Youth Authority

Presented: August 4, 1992

_____
Director

STATE OF CALIFORNIA—YOUTH AND ADULT CORRECTIONAL AGENCY   PETE WILSON, Governor

DEPARTMENT OF THE YOUTH AUTHORITY
4241 Williamsbourgh Drive, Suite 201
Sacramento, California 95823
(916) 427-4816

August 4, 1992

Pat Benedict
P.O. Box 3936
Edmond, Oklahoma 73083-3936

Dear Pat:

This is to thank you for your hard work during the recent All Peace Officers Association summer camp near Big Bear Lake. With dedicated volunteers like you, the camp experience is a success for all of the children and staff as well.

I sincerely appreciate your commitment to this project. I look forward to your participation next year. Barring no earthquakes in that area next summer, Assistant Director Sharon English and I plan to visit the camp and look forward seeing you in action!

Sincerely,

Wm. B. Kolender
Director

cc: Major Beck, Director

Award of Appreciation

to

Marian Marie Benedict

for participation in the
Veterans History Project of the American Folklife Center
of the Library of Congress

January 10, 2012

Presented by:
American Red Cross
Greater Long Beach Chapter
3150 East 29th Street
Long Beach, California 90806

The Secretary of the Navy takes pleasure in presenting the

NAVY COMMENDATION MEDAL to

              COMMANDER MARIAN M. BENEDICT
                     NURSE CORPS
                   UNITED STATES NAVY

for service as set forth in the following

CITATION:

    For exemplary accomplishment as Nurse/Counselor on the Alcohol Rehabilitation Service, Naval Regional Medical Center, Long Beach, California from January 1974 through November 1979. Steadfastly exhibiting perserverance and establishing a proven record of innovation and expertise, Commander Benedict significantly contributed to the mission of the Naval Regional Medical Center. As a highly versatile health care professional, her resolve and expertise were instrumental in the clinical management of alcoholic and co-alcoholic patients, particularly in complicated treatment cases. Commander Benedict has demonstrated expertise in confrontation of untreated alcoholics and this commitment has assured that many dying alcoholics are now well. Commander Benedict's dynamic speaking ability has led her to organize lectures and workshops in most major Naval Regional Medical Centers throughout the world, as well as in many civilian facilities. Commander Benedict's selfless dedication is a credit to herself, the Medical Department, and the United States Navy.

                                         For the Secretary,

                                         THOMAS B. HAYWARD
                                         Admiral, United States Navy
                                         Chief of Naval Operations

DEPARTMENT OF THE NAVY
NAVAL ALCOHOL REHABILITATION CENTER
NAVAL STATION
SAN DIEGO, CALIFORNIA 92136

```
00:GAB:jlb
1650
Ser 324
20 September 1979
```

From: Commanding Officer, Naval Alcohol Rehabilitation Center, San Diego
To: CDR Marian "Pat" BENEDICT, NC, USN

Subj: Letter of Commendation

1. While serving as Staff Nurse at the Alcohol Rehabilitation Service, Naval Regional Medical Center, Long Beach, California, you were assigned additional duties at this command which you willingly and and unselfishly performed. From 1975 to the present, as on on-line trainer, you provided medical information to students in both our Administration, Training, and Advisor Course and our Alcoholism Treatment Specialist Course, in a professional and thorough manner. You have enhanced the skills of hundreds of our students, aiding in making our training course both the professional and effective program that it has become.

2. Speaking for those in the Prevention and Training Department of ARC San Diego, I want to assure you of our warm appreciation and respect for you for the significant contribution you have made to the Navy's alcoholism program. Training modules became living examples as you shared both your personal and professional expertise on the medical aspects of the disease of alcoholism.

3. As Commanding Officer, and on behalf of my entire staff, I commend you for the way you have shared with us, for the joy and competence of that sharing, and for your willingness to give of your personal time and talents to us. Your retirement, while initially a loss to the Navy, can serve to establish greater cooperation between the military and civilian sectors in the fight against alcoholism. The loyalty and enthusiasm you have demonstrated in your work in the field of alcoholism will continue to serve the needs of the alcoholic, and will continue to reflect proudly upon the Navy and its alcoholism effort.

4. We wish you all success and God's speed; and please "Keep Coming Back".

G. A. BUNN

The Surgeon General of the Navy

presents this

CERTIFICATE OF MERIT

to

COMMANDER MARIAN M. BENEDICT
Nurse Corps
United States Navy

For twenty years of loyal and meritorious service in the Nurse Corps of the United States Navy.

Commander Benedict has displayed exceptional qualities of professionalism in both clinical and administrative assignments. Her conscientiousness, leadership and commitment with regard to the Navy's alcoholism treatment and rehabilitative services are without equal. Her performance of duty, personal courage, and extensive community involvement have earned her the respect of both civilian and military associates.

Throughout the years her devotion to the healing arts has been an inspiration to all - reflecting great credit upon herself and the United States Navy.

On the occasion of her retirement, it is a pleasure to record here our appreciation and gratitude and confer upon Commander Benedict this CERTIFICATE OF MERIT in recognition of an exemplary career in the service of our country.

W. P. ARENTZEN
Vice Admiral, Medical Corps
United States Navy

Proof

Made in the USA
Charleston, SC
22 November 2016